FACTS FOR LIFE

Books by His Divine Grace
A. C. Bhaktivedanta Swami Prabhupāda

Bhagavad-gītā As It Is
Śrīmad-Bhāgavatam (with disciples)
Śrī Caitanya-caritāmṛta
Kṛṣṇa, the Supreme Personality of Godhead
Teachings of Lord Caitanya
The Nectar of Devotion
The Nectar of Instruction
Śrī Īśopaniṣad
Light of the Bhāgavata
Easy Journey to Other Planets
Teachings of Lord Kapila, the Son of Devahūti
Teachings of Queen Kuntī
Message of Godhead
The Science of Self-Realization
The Perfection of Yoga
Beyond Birth and Death
On the Way to Kṛṣṇa
Rāja-vidyā: The King of Knowledge
Elevation to Kṛṣṇa Consciousness
Kṛṣṇa Consciousness: The Matchless Gift
Kṛṣṇa Consciousness: The Topmost Yoga System
Perfect Questions, Perfect Answers
Life Comes from Life
The Nārada-bhakti-sūtra (with disciples)
The Mukunda-mālā-stotra (with disciples)
Geetār-gān (Bengali)
Vairāgya-vidyā (Bengali)
Buddhi-yoga (Bengali)
Bhakti-ratna-boli (Bengali)
Back to Godhead magazine (founder)

Books compiled from the teachings of His Divine Grace
A. C. Bhaktivedanta Swami Prabhupāda after his lifetime

Search for Liberation
A Second Chance
The Journey of Self-Discovery
Civilization and Transcendence
The Laws of Nature
Renunciation Through Wisdom
The Quest for Enlightenment
Dharma, the Way of Transcendence
Beyond Illusion and Doubt

Available from: www.krishna.com

FACTS FOR LIFE

Conversations with

His Divine Grace
A. C. Bhaktivedanta Swami Prabhupāda
Founder-*Ācārya* of the International Society for Krishna Consciousness

THE BHAKTIVEDANTA BOOK TRUST

Readers interested in the subject matter of this book are invited to write to one of the following addresses:

Karuna Bhavan
Bankhouse Rd, Lesmahagow
Lanarkshire, ML11 0ES
Tel: +44 (0)1555 894790
Fax: +44 (0)1555 894526
E-mail: karunabhavan@aol.com

ISKCON Reader Services
P.O. Box 730
Watford, WD25 8ZE
E-mail: bhaktivedanta.manor@pamho.net

www.krishna.com

ISBN 91-7149-454-5

Printed in the United Kingdom
2003

Contents

Introduction

In 1965 His Divine Grace A. C. Bhaktivedanta Swami Prabhupāda (popularly known as Śrīla Prabhupāda), founder-*ācārya* of the worldwide Hare Kṛṣṇa movement, left India and travelled to New York City, where he began the International Society for Krishna Consciousness a year later. His purpose was to preach Kṛṣṇa consciousness, the practical and complete process of developing love of God, a process delineated in the Vedic scriptures. Śrīla Prabhupāda's profuse commentated translations on these scriptures certainly establish him as one of the greatest religious scholars of all time. He authoritatively presented the science, philosophy, and pastimes of Kṛṣṇa in more than eighty books, simultaneously establishing the Hare Kṛṣṇa movement as a major religious force throughout the world.

Śrīla Prabhupāda's dynamic presentation of Kṛṣṇa consciousness as a spiritual alternative to a society stripped of spiritual values especially attracted the Western youth. Many of these young people were seeking the true meaning of life and were sick of hedonistic materialism, nihilistic atheism, and sentimental, hypocritical semitheism.

Śrīla Prabhupāda's teachings and his life demonstrate that the message of the ancient *Vedas* is by no means outdated but is completely relevant to every person in every place, especially in the modern age. In the spirit of all true religious teachers, Śrīla Prabhupāda spoke out against materialistic society, which enslaves people in ever-increasing complexities while keeping them blind to their real spiritual needs.

Śrīla Prabhupāda certainly spoke out strongly, clearly, and consistently against the spiritual ills of modern society, but without a trace of malice. He did not criticize anyone indiscriminately, nor did he allow his disciples to do so. In his personal dealings he encouraged the good in others and avoided condemning the bad. He gave all respect and praise to genuine spiritual teachers, such as Jesus Christ. Thus, his aim was not to antagonise or condemn anyone but to wake people up to their actual life of happiness in Kṛṣṇa consciousness.

In mid-1977 Śrīla Prabhupāda became very pleased when, in a column entitled *Śrīla Prabhupāda Speaks Out,* excerpts of his conversations in which he forcefully presented the tenets of Kṛṣṇa consciousness in an informal setting began appearing in *Back to Godhead,* the Hare Kṛṣṇa movement's magazine. This book, a collection of those "Speaks Out" columns, gives the reader the opportunity to take advantage of a pure devotee's perspective on the modern world.

The selections in this book portray Śrīla Prabhupāda in a particular mood. The reader should not think that such a strong tone was the only one Śrīla Prabhupāda employed. Most of the exchanges in this book are conversations between Śrīla Prabhupāda and his intimate disciples. Yet in his general preaching to nondevotees he was philosophically no less compromising, though he may have cast the same thoughts in softer tones. For a view of another side of Śrīla Prabhupāda, the reader new to his works may want to refer to other publications from the Bhaktivedanta Book Trust, such as *Perfect Questions Perfect Answers.*

Śrīla Prabhupāda is a perfect Vedic *sādhu.* One of the meanings of the word *sādhu* is "one who cuts," and readers of this small book will certainly experience a lifetime of illusions being chopped away. *Facts for Life* is provocative, controversial, and to the point. Its conclusions are weighty, and no thoughtful person should refrain from studying it from cover to cover.

Finding Perfect Knowledge in an Imperfect World

This conversation between Śrīla Prabhupāda and Dr. Gregory Benford, a professor of physics at the University of California at Irvine, took place in October of 1973 at the Los Angeles Hare Kṛṣṇa centre.

Dr. Benford: You are probably familiar with what Western theology calls "the problem of evil." Why does evil exist?

Śrīla Prabhupāda: Evil is the absence of good, just as darkness is the absence of sunlight. If you keep yourself always in the light, where is the question of darkness? God is all-good. So if you keep yourself always in God consciousness, then there is no evil.

Dr. Benford: But why was the world created with evil men?

Śrīla Prabhupāda: Why was the police department created? Because there is a necessity. Similarly, some living entities want to enjoy this material world; therefore God creates it. He is just like a father who gives a separate room to his mischievous children to play in. Otherwise, the naughty boys would always disturb him.

Dr. Benford: This world, then, is something like a prison?

Śrīla Prabhupāda: Yes, it is a prison. Therefore, there is suffering here. In the prison house you cannot expect comfort, because unless there is suffering, there is no lesson for the prisoners. That is stated in the *Bhagavad-gītā: duḥkhālayam aśāśvatam. Duḥkhālayam* means "the place for suffering." And *aśāśvatam* means "temporary." You cannot make a compromise and say, "All right, I am suffering, but I don't care about that—I shall remain here." You cannot remain here; you will be kicked out. Now you are thinking that you are an American, you are a great scientist, you are happy, you are getting a good salary. That's all right, but you cannot stay in this post. The day will come when you will be kicked out. And you do not know whether you are going to be an American or a scientist or a cat or dog or demigod. You do not know.

Dr. Benford: I think that I will probably be nothing.

Śrīla Prabhupāda: No, that is another kind of ignorance. Kṛṣṇa explains in the *Bhagavad-gītā* [2.13], *dehino 'smin yathā dehe kaumāraṁ yauvanaṁ jarā/ tathā dehāntara-prāptiḥ:* first you are in the body of a boy, then a young man, and in the future you will be in the body of an old man . . .

Dr. Benford: But after I'm an old man I might be nothing.

Śrīla Prabhupāda: No, no. *Tathā dehāntara-prāptiḥ:* after death you will pass into another body. So you cannot say, "I am going to be nothing." Of course, you may say anything, but the laws are different. You may know the law, or you may not know the law. It doesn't matter; the law will act. For example, if you think, "I will touch the fire—it will not burn me," that is not a fact. It will burn. Similarly, you may think there is nothing after death, but it is not a fact.

Dr. Benford: Why does a person like me—someone who's trying to understand the world rationally—seem to find no way in which to do it?

Śrīla Prabhupāda: You are trying to know things rationally, but you are not going to the proper teacher.

Dr. Benford: But I feel that by studying the world I can acquire knowledge, and there is a way to check that knowledge. You formulate hypotheses, you perform experiments, you verify your ideas, and then you see if you can use these ideas in the practical world.

Śrīla Prabhupāda: That is one more kind of ignorance—because you do not know that you are imperfect.

Dr. Benford: Oh, I know that I'm not perfect.

Śrīla Prabhupāda: Then what is the use of your trying to study the world this way and that way? If you are imperfect, the result will be imperfect.

Dr. Benford: That's true.

Śrīla Prabhupāda: So why waste your time?

Dr. Benford: But there doesn't seem to be any other way of finding knowledge.

Śrīla Prabhupāda: Even for material knowledge, you have to go to the university and consult a professor. Similarly, when you want to learn spiritual knowledge—perfect knowledge—you have to approach a perfect teacher. Then you will get perfect knowledge.

Dr. Benford: But how does one know when the teacher is perfect?

Śrīla Prabhupāda: It is not difficult. A perfect teacher is one who has learned from another perfect teacher.

Dr. Benford: But that merely removes the problem a step.

Śrīla Prabhupāda: No, because there is one perfect teacher—Kṛṣṇa—who is accepted by all classes of teachers. In India we still find the Vedic culture, which is taught by Vedic scholars. And all these Vedic teachers accept Kṛṣṇa as the supreme teacher. They take lessons from Kṛṣṇa and teach that.

Dr. Benford: So anyone I meet who accepts Kṛṣṇa as the perfect teacher—he is a perfect teacher?

Śrīla Prabhupāda: Yes. Anyone who is teaching the teachings of Kṛṣṇa—he is a perfect teacher.

Dr. Benford: Then all the devotees here are perfect teachers?

Śrīla Prabhupāda: Yes, because they are teaching only Kṛṣṇa's teachings, that's all. They may not be perfect. But whatever they are speaking is perfect, because it is taught by Kṛṣṇa.

Dr. Benford: Then you are not perfect?

Śrīla Prabhupāda: No, I am not perfect. None of us claim that we are perfect—we have so many defects. But because we don't speak anything beyond Kṛṣṇa's teachings, our teaching is perfect. We are just like a postman who brings you a money order for one thousand dollars. He is not a rich man, but if he delivers to you the envelope as it is, you are benefited. He is not a rich man, but his perfect dealing—his honest dealing—is perfect. Similarly, we are not perfect; we are full of imperfections. But we don't go beyond the teaching of Kṛṣṇa—that is our process—and therefore our teachings are perfect.

Sense Gratification Is for the Birds

The following conversation between Śrīla Prabhupāda and some of his disciples took place in May of 1974 during a morning walk in Rome.

Śrīla Prabhupāda: *Adānta-gobhir viśatāṁ tamisraṁ punaḥ punaś carvita-carvaṇānām.* Life after life, people are simply trying to enjoy their senses. Life after life, the same thing over and over again. The same eating, the same sleeping, the same sexual intercourse, and the same defending, either as a man or a dog. *Punaḥ punaś carvita-carvaṇānām:* again and again, chewing the chewed. Whether you become a demigod or a dog, in the material world everyone is given the facilities for these four things: eating, sleeping, having sexual intercourse, and defending.

Actually, if some danger were to come now, we humans might be victims, but a bird would immediately fly away. So the bird has better facility for defence. Is it not? Suppose all of a sudden a car came directly at us. We would be killed. We could not do anything, but even the smallest bird—"Hut! I'm leaving!" He can do that. Is it not? So his defensive measures are better than ours.

Similarly, if we wanted to have sex, we would have to arrange for that—find out some mate and a suitable time and place. But the female bird is always around the male bird, at any time. Take the sparrows or the pigeons. Have you seen it? Immediately they are ready for sex. And what does the bird do about eating? "Oh, there is some fruit." Immediately the bird can eat. And sleeping is also easy and convenient.

So these facilities—don't think that they are available only in your skyscrapers. They are available for the birds and the beasts. It is not that unless you have got a very nice apartment in the skyscraper, you cannot have all these facilities of eating, sleeping, defending, and having sex. You can have them in any material body, in any species: *viṣayaḥ khalu sarvataḥ syāt. Viṣaya* means the facilities for material sense enjoyment. Our process is *viṣaya chāḍiyā, se rase majiyā.* One has to give up this unsatisfying material enjoyment and relish transcendental bliss, the taste of spiritual enjoyment. It is enjoyment on a different platform.

But today people are so befooled by the bodily concept of life that their only enjoyment is this material, so-called enjoyment. So the scriptures advise, "This temporary, inferior enjoyment is available in any form of material life—either as a man or as a bird or as a beast." Why are you repeatedly going after this same unsatisfying enjoyment in all these different species of life? *Punaḥ punaś carvita-carvaṇānām:* "In all these different forms, again and again you are doing the same stupid, unsatisfying thing."

But *matir na kṛṣṇeărataḥ svato vā:* those who are befooled by material sensual enjoyment cannot become Kṛṣṇa conscious, by their own endeavour or even by instruction from a spiritual master. And *mitho 'bhipadyeta:* these foolish people may hold many conferences and meetings to inquire, "What are the problems of life?"—but still they cannot take to the process of Kṛṣṇa consciousness.

Why? *Gṛha-vratānām.* As long as they have got this determination—"We shall be happy in this material world"—they cannot take to Kṛṣṇa consciousness. *Gṛha* means "home" and also "body." Those who are trying to be happy within this material body—they cannot take to Kṛṣṇa consciousness, because *adānta-gobhiḥ:* their senses are so uncontrolled. Therefore these people must repeatedly undergo the ordeal of chewing the chewed. Again and again, the same sensual enjoyment: eating, sleeping, mating, and defending.

Disciple: So our task is to convince people that they can't be happy in the material world?

Śrīla Prabhupāda: Yes. And they have already got very convincing experience. Daily they are founding so many parties, manufacturing so many means and plans and this and that, but still they are not happy. And yet they are such great fools that in spite of being repeatedly baffled, still, they are chewing what they have already chewed—the same thing all over again, in somewhat different forms.

What is the difference between the communists and capitalists? After all, both groups are simply looking after how they can make things into a better arrangement for their own sensual enjoyment. The two groups are fighting, but everyone's aim is *gṛha-vratānām:* "We shall remain within this material world and be happy here."

Disciple: The idea is, if we can get enough food and sex, we will be happy.

Śrīla Prabhupāda: That's all. And then people become impotent. And they beg the doctor, "Give me some sex medicine." You see? *Punaḥ punaś carvita-carvaṇānām.* Chewing the same old tired thing. And when they feel disgusted with sex at home: "Let us go to the prostitute. Let us go to the naked dance." They have no other ideas. So this class of men cannot take to Kṛṣṇa consciousness. First of all, one must be in knowledge—"I am not anything of this material world. I am spirit soul.

My happiness is in the spiritual world." Then he is a real human being and he can make spiritual advancement.

So the next question is, "How can one become interested in the spirit soul and Kṛṣṇa consciousness?" How? This is the question. Animals and people like animals cannot become interested.

naiṣāṁ matis tāvad urukramāṅghriṁ
spṛśaty anarthāpagamo yad-arthaḥ
mahīyasāṁ pāda-rajo-'bhiṣekaṁ
niṣkiñcanānāṁ na vṛṇīta yāvat

The *Śrīmad-Bhāgavatam* [7.5.32] says, "The consciousness of these rascals and fools cannot be turned toward the lotus feet of Lord Śrī Kṛṣṇa, who acts wonderfully, until they touch their heads to the lotus feet of a devotee of the Lord who is *niṣkiñcana,* who has nothing to gain in this material world and is simply interested in Kṛṣṇa." If you get the opportunity of touching your head to the lotus feet or even the dust of the lotus feet of such a great devotee, your spiritual advancement is possible. Otherwise, it is not. The dust of the lotus feet of a great devotee can help you.

Can We Put a Date on Wisdom?

This exchange between Śrīla Prabhupāda and a British student took place during an early-morning walk in London in August of 1973.

Śrīla Prabhupāda: The message of Kṛṣṇa consciousness comes from the spiritual world. It is not of this material world. Therefore sometimes people may misunderstand it. So we have to explain it nicely. They cannot even understand what is the soul. Big, big scientists. Big, big philosophers. They have no information of the spirit and the spiritual world. Therefore, sometimes they find it very difficult to understand.

Guest: Lately I've been doing some research on the dating of the *Vedas.* You know, some archaeologists maintain that the evidence from the Harappa dig and Mohenjo-Daro show the dating of the *Vedas* in fact to be a great deal later than previously thought. This would seem to deprive the *Vedas* of a certain amount of authority, because they no longer would appear to be the most ancient religious scriptures in the world.

Śrīla Prabhupāda: *Veda* does not mean religion. *Veda* means knowledge. So if you can trace out the history of knowledge, then you can trace out the date for the origin of the *Vedas.* Can you trace out when knowledge began? Can you trace it out?

Guest: I wouldn't think we could.

Śrīla Prabhupāda: So how can you trace out the history

of the *Vedas? Veda* means knowledge. So first of all find out from which date knowledge began. Then you find out the age of the *Vedas.*

The history of the *Vedas* began from the date of the creation of this material world. No one can give the date of the creation. The creation begins with the birth of Brahmā, and you cannot calculate even the length of Brahmā's one day. During Brahmā's night, the universe is devastated to some extent, and during his daytime, creation takes place again. There are two kinds of devastations. One devastation takes place during the night of Brahmā, and one final devastation annihilates the entire cosmic manifestation. But these teeny people are speculating about the dates of the *Vedas.* That is ludicrous.

There are many microbes that grow in the evening and die just as the day is beginning. One night is their whole span of life. So our life is like that. What history can you write? Therefore, we receive Vedic knowledge from Vedic authorities.

One should not be a frog philosopher. Do you know about frog philosophy? Dr. Frog had never seen the Atlantic Ocean, and somebody informed him, "Oh, I have seen such a vast mass of water."

So Dr. Frog said, "Oh, is it bigger than this well?"

Guest: Yes, it was beyond his conception.

Śrīla Prabhupāda: Yes. So these scholars are like frogs rotting in their wells. What can they possibly understand of the Vedic knowledge?

Guest: Yes, I see. To change the subject, I wonder whether you feel that the *Vedas* affirm that the most true form of life, the most pure form of life, is one that's lived alongside nature, not against nature, as we seem to be doing in our urban setting.

Śrīla Prabhupāda: Oh, yes. Real life means you have to

minimise your bodily activities so that you can save time and devote yourself to spiritual understanding. That is real life. And the present civilisation based on the bodily concept of life is animal life. It is not civilised life. *Athāto brahma-jijñāsā.* Civilised life begins when one is so much advanced that he enquires about the spirit soul. But when there is no such enquiry, when people cannot inquire what is spirit soul, they are like cats and dogs. Vedic life teaches one to become as free as possible from bodily disturbances. Therefore, Vedic education begins with *brahmacarya,* celibacy. You see? But these rascals cannot check their sex life. Their philosophy is that you should go on with sex life unrestrictedly and when there is pregnancy kill the child.

Guest: Yes.

Śrīla Prabhupāda: That is their rascal philosophy. They have no idea that by training one can forget sex life. And if you forget sex life, where is the question of abortion? But they cannot do that. Therefore it is said, *adānta-gobhir viśatāṁ tamisraṁ:* by unrestricted sense enjoyment they are gradually going down to the level of animal life.

A person who indulges in abortion, killing the baby in the womb, will be put into a womb in his next life, and somebody will kill him. As many babies as he has killed, he'll have to accept that many lives and be killed. So for hundreds of years it will be impossible for him to see daylight. He'll remain in the womb and be killed. People don't know nature's laws. One cannot violate nature's laws as one can the state laws. Suppose you kill somebody—you can escape by trick. But you cannot escape nature's law. As many times as you have killed, that many times you must be killed within the womb. That is nature's law.

Guest: Only last week I was talking to a nurse who works on an abortion ward in one of the main London hospitals. It's terrible. Some of the fetuses are in such an advanced state of development that clearly life is a strong possibility.

Śrīla Prabhupāda: There is no question of possibility. Life begins from the very beginning of sex. The living entity is very small. By nature's law, according to his *karma*, he's sent into the father's semen and injected into the mother's womb. The sperm and egg cells from the man and woman emulsify and form a body that is just like a pea. Then that pealike form develops gradually. This is all described in the Vedic literature. The first stage is the manifestation of nine holes—for the ears, eyes, nostrils, mouth, genitals, and anus.

Then the senses gradually develop, and by six and a half months everything is complete, and the living entity's consciousness comes back. Prior to the formation of the body, the living entity remains unconscious, like in anaesthesia. Then he dreams, and then gradually comes to consciousness. At that time he becomes very much reluctant to come out, but nature gives him a push, and he comes out. This is the process of birth.

This is Vedic knowledge. In the Vedic literature you'll find everything perfectly described. Therefore, how can the *Vedas* be subject to history? But the difficulty is that we are speaking of things that are spiritual. Therefore it is sometimes difficult for the gross materialists to understand. They are so dull-headed that they cannot understand.

On a Society Without Brains

The following conversation between Śrīla Prabhupāda and Charles Hennis, of the International Labour Organization, took place in Geneva in May of 1974.

Mr. Hennis: I work for the International Labour Organization, which is a part of the United Nations family. We're concerned with the protection and welfare of all labourers in practically all nations in the world.

Śrīla Prabhupāda: The Vedic literature describes four social classes—intelligent, administrative, mercantile, labourer. The labourers act as the legs of the social body, but legs must be guided by the head. That head of the social body is the intelligent class. The United Nations is taking care of the social body's legs, but what are they doing for the brain—the intelligent class?

Mr. Hennis: We want to see that the labourers have their proper share in society's economic rewards.

Śrīla Prabhupāda: But my point is that if you neglect the head of society, then in spite of your attention to the legs, things will not go very nicely—because the brain will not be in order.

Mr. Hennis: But this is also an important aspect of society, don't you think? We aim to improve the lot of the workers of the world.

Śrīla Prabhupāda: In America the labourer class is very highly paid, but because they are not directed by a brain, by an intelligent class, they simply spend their money on drinking.

Mr. Hennis: The fact that a good thing is abused doesn't make it bad.

Śrīla Prabhupāda: The point is that everyone should be guided by the brain. That is the only way to organise society. What is the value in working hard like an ass, without any intelligence?

Mr. Hennis: You can't force a man to use his brain.

Śrīla Prabhupāda: Therefore, the United Nations should support a class of ideal intelligent men who will act as the brain of society and guide the others so that everyone becomes happy.

Mr. Hennis: I think you'll find that in every society throughout the world there is a priestly class, a class of philosophical leaders.

Śrīla Prabhupāda: Priestly class! The Bible says, "Thou shalt not kill." But the priests have amended this to suit their own whims. They have sanctioned killing by allowing thousands of huge slaughterhouses for killing innocent animals. How can such so-called priests guide? I have asked so many Christian gentlemen and priests about this: "Your Bible teaches, 'Thou shalt not kill.' Why are you violating this commandment?" They give me vague answers. They have not even taught the people what is sinful. That means a lack of brains in society.

Mr. Hennis: My organisation is not directly concerned with people's brains.

Śrīla Prabhupāda: Your organisation may not be directly concerned, but if human society is brainless, then no matter what organisations you make, people will never become happy. If people are not taught by the intelligent class of society how to discriminate between pious and sinful activities, then they are no better than the animals.

Mr. Hennis: Of course, when you speak of the distinction between pious activities and sinful activities . . .
Śrīla Prabhupāda: They see no such distinction anymore. But in our Kṛṣṇa consciousness society I instruct my students from the very beginning to avoid sinful activities. They must give up completely all meat-eating, gambling, illicit sex, and intoxication. And now just compare their character and behaviour with anyone else's. Even the Christian priests are surprised. They say, "These boys are our boys. How is it that before joining your movement they never came to church, but now they are mad after God?" In the streets, people ask, "Are you Americans?"

You see, everything can be rectified by proper guidance. But if there is no brain in society, you can manufacture so many organisations, but people will go on suffering. That is nature's law: if the people are sinful, they have to suffer.
Mr. Hennis: I don't think that you can expect an international organisation to indoctrinate people . . .
Śrīla Prabhupāda: Why not? It *should* be international—everyone. The United Nations is meant for international activity, so our proposal is that the United Nations maintain an international organisation of first-class intelligent men to act as the brains of society. Then people can be happy. But if you want to keep the hands and legs working without direction, without a brain, then you will never be successful.
Mr. Hennis: You know, I think of myself as a servant of mankind, with a view toward helping people to understand one another and the world a little better. I'm trying now to organise workers' education programs . . .
Śrīla Prabhupāda: But please try to understand. I'm stressing on the point of society's brain. If there is no ideal class of men, if the brain is not in order, then no

amount of education or organisation you do will be successful. The United Nations is an organisation for all human society, but they have no department that can actually be called the brain organisation.

Mr. Hennis: That's true.

Śrīla Prabhupāda: That is my point.

Mr. Hennis: We are only servants of the leaders of our member states. If Mr. Nixon and all the other heads of state don't have brains, then I'm afraid the United Nations can't do anything to give them brains.

Śrīla Prabhupāda: Then your big organisation is just decoration for a dead body. A body with no brain is a dead body. You may decorate a dead body to your full satisfaction, but what is the use? Without a brain, a class of men in society to instruct the others what is right and what is wrong, then the social body is dead, or headless. And whatever work you do will simply be useless decoration for a dead body.

Plain Living, High Thinking

The following conversation between Śrīla Prabhupāda and some of his disciples took place in New Vrindaban, West Virginia, in June of 1976.

Śrīla Prabhupāda: The Western civilisation is a nasty civilisation, artificially increasing the necessities of life. For example, take the electric light. The electric light requires a generator, and to run the generator you need petroleum. As soon as the petroleum supply is stopped, everything will stop. But to get petroleum you have to painstakingly search it out and bore deep into the earth, sometimes in the middle of the ocean. This is *ugra-karma,* horrible work. The same purpose can be served by growing some castor seeds, pressing out the oil, and putting the oil into a pot with a wick. We admit that you have improved the lighting system with electricity, but to improve from the castor-oil lamp to the electric lamp you have to work very hard. You have to go to the middle of the ocean and drill and then draw out the petroleum, and in this way the real goal of your life is missed. You are in a precarious position, constantly dying and taking birth in various species of life. How to get free of this cycle of birth and death—this is your real problem. And this problem is meant to be solved in the human life. You have advanced intelligence for self-realisation, but instead of using your advanced intelligence for self-realisation, you are utilising it to improve from the castor-oil lamp to the electric lamp. That's all.

Disciple: People would say that your suggestion is impractical. Besides, electricity does many other things besides produce light. Most of our modern comforts depend more or less on electricity.

Śrīla Prabhupāda: In this life you may be living very comfortably, but in the next life you might become a dog.

Disciple: People don't believe that.

Śrīla Prabhupāda: Whether they believe it or not, it is a fact. For example, a boy does not know that he is going to grow into a young man, but his mother and father know. If the boy says, "No, I'm not going to become a young man," that is childish. The father and mother know that the boy will grow into a young man and that they should educate him so he can be properly situated. This is the guardians' duty.

Similarly, when we talk of transmigration of the soul, a rascal may say, "I don't believe in it," but it is still a fact A rascal, a madman, may say transmigration is not a fact, but the real fact is that he'll have to accept another body according to the quality of his endeavour in this life: *kāraṇaṁ guṇa-saṅgo 'sya sad-asad-yoni-janmasu.*

Disciple: What if someone says, "This life of growing the castor seeds is very difficult, and farming in general is very difficult. It is easier to go to the factory for eight hours, come home with my money, and enjoy."

Śrīla Prabhupāda: You may enjoy, but by enjoying you forget your real goal in life. Is that intelligent? You have been given the human body to improve your next life. Suppose you become a dog in your next life. Is that success? You must know the science of Kṛṣṇa consciousness. Then, instead of becoming a dog, you will become like God.

Disciple: Once, at John Lennon's estate in London, you said that the tractor is the cause of so much of the trouble today. It took all the work from the young men and forced them to go to the city for work, and they became entangled in sense gratification. I've noticed that life in the country is simpler, more peaceful. It's easier to think of spiritual life.

Śrīla Prabhupāda: Yes. The country is less disturbing, less taxing on the brain. Just work a little for your food, and the rest of the time engage yourself in Kṛṣṇa consciousness. This is ideal life.

[*Śrīla Prabhupāda holds up a flower.*] See the minute fibres in this flower. Can anyone manufacture this in a factory—such small fibres? And how brilliant the colour is! If you study only one flower, you become God conscious. There is a machine that you call "nature," and from this machine everything is coming. But who has built this machine?

Disciple: In London you said people don't know that the flowers are painted by Kṛṣṇa—with thought.

Śrīla Prabhupāda: Yes. Do you think that without an artist the flowers can come out so beautiful? This is foolish. What is nature? It is Kṛṣṇa's machine. Everything is being done by the machine of Kṛṣṇa.

So improve your mode of living at New Vrindaban. Live in an open place, produce your own food grains, produce your own milk, save time, chant Hare Kṛṣṇa. Plain living, high thinking: ideal life. But if you increase the artificial necessities of your life—your so-called comforts—and forget your real work of Kṛṣṇa consciousness, that is suicidal. We want to stop this suicidal policy. Of course, we don't insist that people stop the modern advancement of technology. We just present the simple formula given by Śrī Caitanya Mahāprabhu:* Chant Hare Kṛṣṇa. Even in your technological factory you can chant. What is the difficulty? You can go on pushing the buttons on your machine and simultaneously chant Hare Kṛṣṇa, Hare Kṛṣṇa, Kṛṣṇa Kṛṣṇa, Hare Hare/ Hare Rāma, Hare Rāma, Rāma Rāma, Hare Hare.

Disciple: And if people take up the chanting, gradually they will give up the technology?

Śrīla Prabhupāda: Of course.

Disciple: So you're sowing the seeds of their destruction.

Śrīla Prabhupāda: No, not destruction; rather *con*struction. The repetition of birth and death, the constant change of bodies—this is destruction. But by our method, you live forever—*tyaktvā dehaṁ punar janma naiti:* you don't get another material body. But without Kṛṣṇa consciousness, *tathā dehāntara-prāptiḥ:* you have to accept another body, which means suffering. So, which is better? To accept material bodies, one after another, or to accept no more material bodies? If we finish our suffering with this body, that is intelligent, but if we create another body for further suffering, that is unintelligent. But unless you understand Kṛṣṇa, you have to accept another body. There is no alternative.

---

* Śrī Caitanya Mahāprabhu is Lord Kṛṣṇa Himself in the role of His own devotee. He appeared in the late fifteenth century to spread love of God through the chanting of the holy names.

Scientific Proof of the Soul

The following conversation between Śrīla Prabhupāda and an Indian doctor took place in September of 1973 at the Hare Kṛṣṇa centre in London.

Doctor: Can you scientifically prove that the soul exists? I mean, is it purely a matter of belief, or . . .

Śrīla Prabhupāda: No, it is a scientific fact. Our science is perfect, because we are receiving knowledge from the perfect source, Kṛṣṇa. And modern so-called science is imperfect, because the scientists' knowledge is received from imperfect sources. However great a scientist you may be, you have to admit that your senses are imperfect.

Doctor: Yes.

Śrīla Prabhupāda: So, imperfect senses can give only imperfect knowledge. What you are calling scientific knowledge is bogus, because the men who have produced that knowledge are imperfect. How can you expect perfect knowledge from an imperfect person?

Doctor: It's a question of degree.

Śrīla Prabhupāda: My point is that if you are unable to give perfect knowledge, what is the use of taking knowledge from you?

Doctor: Yes, I accept that view. But how do you prove that the soul exists?

Śrīla Prabhupāda: You take information from the perfect source, Kṛṣṇa, or from Kṛṣṇa's representative, who repeats the *words* of Kṛṣṇa. That is our process of proof. *Evaṁ paramparā-prāptam:* "Transcendental knowledge must be received in disciplic succession." We don't accept knowledge from a rascal; we accept knowledge from Kṛṣṇa, the Supreme. I may be a rascal, but because I am receiving knowledge from the perfect source and repeating that, whatever I say is perfect.

A child may be ignorant—but because he has learned that a certain article is called "table", when he says "Father, this is a table," his words are perfect. Similarly, if you hear from the perfect person and believe that, then your knowledge is perfect. Kṛṣṇa says, *tathā dehāntara-prāptiḥ:* "After death the spirit soul enters another material body." We accept it. We don't require proof from a so-called scientist, who is imperfect.

Doctor: So the question of belief comes first.

Śrīla Prabhupāda: It is not belief; it is fact.

Doctor: Yes, but how do you prove that fact?

Śrīla Prabhupāda: That Kṛṣṇa says so is proof.

Doctor: [*very sarcastically*] "It has been said by Kṛṣṇa." But . . .

Śrīla Prabhupāda: That is our Vedic proof. Whenever we say something, we immediately quote from the Vedic literature to support it. This is the process of proof, which is just like that in the law court. When a lawyer is arguing in court, he must quote from previous judgments. Then his argument will be accepted by the judge as legal proof. Similarly, as soon as we say something, we immediately support it by quoting from the Vedic literature. That is the way of proof in spiritual matters. Otherwise, what are the scriptures for? If they are merely products of mental speculation, what is the use of these books? Of course, the Vedic literature also presents the Absolute Truth with all logic and reasoning. For example, in the *Bhagavad-gītā* [2.13] Kṛṣṇa says,

> *dehino 'smin yathā dehe kaumāraṁ yauvanaṁ jarā*
> *tathā dehāntara-prāptir dhīras tatra na muhyati*

"The soul is changing his body from childhood to youth and from youth to old age. Similarly, the soul enters another body at death." Where is the illogical presentation? This is scientific. For an intelligent man, this is scientific proof. And if he's still dull-headed, what can be done?

Doctor: But the soul is invisible. How can you be so sure it exists?

Śrīla Prabhupāda: Just because something is invisible doesn't mean we can't know it exists. The subtle body of mind, intelligence, and ego is also invisible to you, but you know that the subtle body is there. We have two kinds of bodies: a gross body of earth, water, fire, air, and ether, and a subtle body of mind, intelligence, and ego. You can see the body of earth, water, and so on, but can you see the subtle body? Can you see the mind? Can you see the intelligence? Yet everyone knows you have a mind and I have a mind.

Doctor: These are something abstract, you know.

Śrīla Prabhupāda: No, not abstract. They are subtle matter, that's all. You simply have no eyes to see them.

Doctor: Well, at present we have three methods for studying the intelligence . . .

Śrīla Prabhupāda: Anyway, you accept that the subtle body exists even though you cannot see it. That is my point. Similarly, the soul exists even though you cannot see it. The soul is covered by the subtle and the gross bodies. What is known as death is the annihilation of the gross body. The subtle body remains and carries the soul to a place where he can again grow another gross material body just suitable for fulfilling the desires of his mind.

English guest: You mean the subtle body and the soul are the same thing?

Śrīla Prabhupāda: No, the soul is different from the

subtle body. The soul is finer than intelligence. These things are all explained in the *Bhagavad-gītā* [3.42]:

indriyāṇi parāṇy āhur indriyebhyaḥ paraṁ manaḥ
manasas tu parā buddhir yo buddheḥ paratas tu saḥ

First of all, in the gross understanding, we are aware of only the senses of the body. Those who are like animals think that the senses are all in all. They do not understand that the senses are controlled by the mind. If one's mind is distorted, then his senses cannot work; he is a madman. So the controller of the senses is the mind. And above the mind is the intelligence. And above the intelligence is the soul.

We cannot see even the mind and intelligence, so how can we see the soul? But the soul has his existence, his magnitude. And if one has no understanding of the spirit soul, he is no better than an animal, because he is identifying himself with his gross and subtle material bodies.

The Night-and-Day Dream

This conversation between Śrīla Prabhupāda and a university student took place in Los Angeles in January of 1974.

Student: In your books you say this world is like a dream.
Śrīla Prabhupāda: Yes, it is a dream.
Student: How is it a dream?
Śrīla Prabhupāda: For example, last night you had some dream, but now it has no value. It is gone. And again, tonight when you sleep, you'll forget all these things and dream. You won't remember, when you are dreaming tonight, "I've got my house; I've got my wife." You'll forget it all. So all of this is a dream.
Student: Is it true, or is it not true?
Śrīla Prabhupāda: How could it be true? At night you forget it. Do you remember when you sleep that you've got your wife and you're sleeping on a bed? When you have gone some three thousand miles away and seen something totally different in your dream, do you remember that you've got a place to reside in?
Student: No.
Śrīla Prabhupāda: So this is a dream. Tonight, what you are seeing now will become only a dream, just as what you saw last night—now you know it was only a dream. So both are dreams. You are simply a visitor, that's all. You are seeing this dream and that dream. You, the spirit soul, are factual. But your material body and the material surroundings you are seeing—this is a dream.

Student: But I have the impression that this experience is true and my dream is not true. What is the difference . . .

Śrīla Prabhupāda: No. This experience is all untrue! How could it be true? If it were true, how could you forget it at night? How could you forget it, if it were true? At night do you remember all this?

Student: I don't remember.

Śrīla Prabhupāda: Then—how could it be true? Just as you don't remember the dream you saw last night and so you call it a "dream," similarly this experience—because you forget it at night—this is also a dream . . .

Student: But I have the impress . . .

Śrīla Prabhupāda: This is a daydream; that is a night dream. That's all. When you dream at night, then you perceive that as being real. Yes. You think that is real. It is a dream, but you are crying, "There is a tiger! Tiger! Tiger!" Where is the tiger? But you are seeing it as fact—a tiger. "I'm being killed by a tiger!" But where is the tiger? Or you dream you are embracing some beautiful girl. Where is that beautiful girl? But actually it is happening.

Student: It is happening?

Śrīla Prabhupāda: In one sense it is happening, because there is discharge of semen. Nocturnal emission. But where is that girl? Is it not a dream? But similarly, this so-called real-life experience is also a dream. You are getting the impression of factuality, but it is a dream. Therefore it is called *māyā-sukhāya,* illusory happiness. Your night-time happiness and your daytime happiness are the same thing. At night you are dreaming you are embracing a nice, beautiful girl, and there is no such thing. Similarly, in the daytime also, whatever "advancement" you are making—this is also like that. *Māyā-sukhāya:* you are dreaming, "This process will make me happy" or "That process will make me happy," but the whole process is only a dream. You are taking this daydream as reality because the duration is long. At night when you dream, the duration is just half an hour. But this daydream lasts for twelve hours or more. That is the difference. This is a twelve-hour dream, and that is a half-hour dream—but actually both of them are dreams. Because one is a twelve-hour dream, you are accepting it as real. That is called illusion.

Student: Illusion.

Śrīla Prabhupāda: Yes . . . You are making a distinction between an animal and yourself, but you are forgetting that just as the animal will die, you will also die. So where is your advancement? Will you remain forever? You will also die. So where is your advancement over an animal? That is stated in the Vedic literatures. *Āhāra-nidrā-bhaya-maithunaṁ ca sāmānyam etat paśubhir narāṇām:* this business—eating, sleeping, sex life, and defending—this is also the animal's business, and you are doing the same. So how are you distinct from an animal? You will die; the animal will die. But if you say, "I will die after one hundred years, and this ant will die after one hour," that does not mean that you are in reality. It is a question of time. Or take this huge universe—it will all be destroyed. As your body will be destroyed, this universe will also be destroyed. Annihilation. Dissolution. Nature's way—the whole thing will be dissolved.

Therefore, it is a dream. It is a long-duration dream, that's all. Nothing else. But the advantage of having this human body is that in this dream you can realise the reality—God. That is the advantage. So if you don't take advantage of this dream, then you are missing everything.

Student: So I'm half asleep?

Śrīla Prabhupāda: Yes. This is the situation. Therefore, the Vedic literatures say, *uttiṣṭha:* "Get up! Get up!" *Jāgrata:* "Become awakened!" *Prāpya varān nibodhata:* "Now you've got the opportunity, utilise it." *Tamasi mā jyotir gama:* "Don't stay in darkness; come to the light." These are Vedic injunctions. And we are teaching the same thing. "Reality is here—Kṛṣṇa. Don't remain in this dark place. Come to this higher consciousness."

The "Morals" of Meat-Eating

The following conversation between Śrīla Prabhupāda and Cardinal Jean Danielou took place in Paris in August of 1973.

Śrīla Prabhupāda: Jesus Christ said, "Thou shalt not kill." So why is it that the Christian people are engaged in animal-killing and meat-eating?

Cardinal Danielou: Certainly in Christianity it is forbidden to kill. But we believe that there is a difference between the life of a human being and the life of a beast. The life of a human being is sacred because man is made in the image of God. Therefore, to kill a human being is forbidden in the Bible.

Śrīla Prabhupāda: But the Bible does not simply say, "Thou shalt not kill the human being." It says broadly, "Thou shalt not kill."

Cardinal Danielou: It is necessary for man to kill animals in order for him to have food to eat.

Śrīla Prabhupāda: No. Man can eat fruits, vegetables, and grains and drink milk.

Cardinal Danielou: No flesh?

Śrīla Prabhupāda: No. Human beings are meant to eat vegetarian food. The tiger does not come to eat your fruits. His prescribed food is animal flesh. But man's food is vegetables, fruits, grains, and milk products. So how can you say that animal-killing is not a sin?

Cardinal Danielou: We believe it is a question of

motivation. If the killing of an animal is for giving food to the hungry, then it is justified.

Śrīla Prabhupāda: But consider the cow: We drink her milk, and therefore she is our mother. Do you agree?

Cardinal Danielou: Yes, surely.

Śrīla Prabhupāda: So if the cow is your mother, how can you support killing her? You take the milk from her, and when she's old and cannot give you milk, you cut her throat. Is that a very humane proposal? In India those who are meat-eaters are advised to kill some lower animals like goats, pigs, or even buffalo. But cow-killing is the greatest sin. In preaching Kṛṣṇa consciousness we ask people not to eat any kind of meat, and my disciples strictly follow this principle. But if, under certain circumstances, others are obliged to eat meat, then they should eat the flesh of some lower animal. Don't kill cows. It is the greatest sin. And as long as a man is sinful, he cannot understand God. The human being's business is to understand God and to love Him. But if you remain sinful, you will never be able to understand God—what to speak of loving Him.

When there is no other food, someone may eat meat in order to keep from starving. That is all right. But it is most sinful to regularly maintain slaughterhouses just to satisfy your tongue. Actually, you will not even have a human society until this cruel practice of maintaining slaughterhouses is stopped. And although animal-killing may sometimes be necessary for survival, at least the mother animal, the cow, should not be killed. That is simply human decency. In the Kṛṣṇa consciousness movement our practice is that we don't allow the killing of any animals. Kṛṣṇa says, *patraṁ puṣpaṁ phalaṁ toyaṁ yo me bhaktyā prayacchati:* "Vegetables, fruits, milk, and grains should be offered to Me in devotion." [*Bhagavad-gītā* 9.26] We take only *prasādam,* the remnants of

Kṛṣṇa's food. The trees offer us many varieties of fruits, but the trees are not killed. Of course, one living entity is food for another living entity, but that does not mean you can kill your mother for food. Cows are innocent; they give us milk. You take their milk—and then you kill them in the slaughterhouse. This is sinful.

Disciple: Śrīla Prabhupāda, Christianity's sanction of meat-eating is based on the view that lower species of life do not have a soul like the human being's.

Śrīla Prabhupāda: That is foolishness. First of all, we have to understand the evidence of the soul's presence within the body. Then we can see whether the human being has a soul and the cow does not. What are the different characteristics of the cow and the man? If we find a difference in characteristics, then we can say that in the animal there is no soul. But if we see that the animal and the human being have the same characteristics, then how can you say that the animal has no soul? The general symptoms are that the animal eats, you eat; the animal sleeps, you sleep; the animal mates, you mate; the animal defends, you defend. Where is the difference?

Cardinal Danielou: We admit that in the animal there may be the same type of biological existence as in man, but there is no soul. We believe that the soul is a human soul.

Śrīla Prabhupāda: Our *Bhagavad-gītā* says *sarva-yoniṣu:* "In all species of life the soul exists."

Cardinal Danielou: But the life of man is sacred. Human beings think on a higher platform than the animals do.

Śrīla Prabhupāda: What is that higher platform? The animal eats to maintain his body, and you also eat in order to maintain your body. The cow eats grass in the field, and the human being eats meat from a huge slaughterhouse full of modem machines. But just because you have big machines and a ghastly scene, while the animal simply eats grass, this does not mean that you are so advanced that only within your body is there a soul, and that there is not a soul within the body of the animal. That is illogical. We can see that the basic characteristics are the same in the animal and the human being.

Cardinal Danielou: But only in human beings do we find a metaphysical search for the meaning of life.

Śrīla Prabhupāda: Yes. So metaphysically search out why you believe that there is no soul within the animal—that is metaphysics. If you are thinking metaphysically, that is all right. But if you are thinking like an animal, then what is the use of your metaphysical study? Metaphysical means "above the physical," or in other words, spiritual. In the *Bhagavad-gītā* Kṛṣṇa says, *sarva-yoniṣu kaunteya:* "In every living being there is a spirit soul." That is metaphysical understanding.

Women's Liberation

This exchange between Śrīla Prabhupāda and a woman newspaper reporter took place at Chicago's Hare Kṛṣṇa centre in July of 1975.

Reporter: What advice do you have for women who do not want to be subordinate to men?
Śrīla Prabhupāda: It is not my advice but the advice of the Vedic literatures—that a woman should be chaste and faithful to her husband.
Reporter: What should we do in the United States? We're trying to make women equal with men.
Śrīla Prabhupāda: You will never be equal with men, because in so many respects your functions are different. Why do you say artificially they're equal with man's? The wife has to become pregnant, not the husband. How can you change this? Both the husband and the wife will become pregnant—is it possible?
Reporter: *[No reply]*
Śrīla Prabhupāda: Is it possible?
Reporter: No, it is not.
Śrīla Prabhupāda: Then by nature one has to function differently from the other.
Reporter: Why does this mean that women have to be subordinate—just because they bear children and men can't?
Śrīla Prabhupāda: By nature, as soon as you get children you require support from your husband. Otherwise, you are in difficulty.

Reporter: Many women with children have no support from their husband. They have no . . .

Śrīla Prabhupāda: Then they have to take support from others. You cannot deny that. The government is giving them support. Today the government is embarrassed. If the husband supported the wife and children, the government would be relieved of so much welfare expenditure. So that is a problem.

Reporter: What happens when women support men?

Śrīla Prabhupāda: First of all, try to understand that you are dependent. After a man and a woman unite, there are children. And if the man goes away, you are embarrassed—the woman is embarrassed. Why? The poor woman is embarrassed with the child—she has to beg from the government. So do you think it is a very nice thing? The Vedic idea is that a woman should be married to a man, and the man should take care of that woman and the children—independently—so that they do not become a burden to the government or to the public.

Reporter: Do you think that the social unrest . . .

Śrīla Prabhupāda: I am thinking like this. You give me the answer! Simply you go on questioning. I will question you. Do you think this burden to the government and the public is good?

Reporter: I don't understand what you're saying.

Śrīla Prabhupāda: Every year the government has to pay out millions of dollars in aid to dependent children. Do you think that this burden caused when the husband goes away from the wife—this *burden* to the government and the people—is good?

Reporter: No.

Śrīla Prabhupāda: That has happened because the woman does not agree to be subordinate. She wants "equal freedom."

Reporter: And if women were subordinate to men, I suppose that would solve all of our problems?

Śrīla Prabhupāda: Yes. The husband wants that his wife should be subordinate—faithful to him. Then he's ready to take charge. Man's mentality and woman's mentality are different. So, if the woman agrees to remain faithful and subordinate to the man, then family life will be peaceful. Otherwise the husband goes away, the woman is embarrassed with the children, and it becomes a burden to the government and the people in general.

Reporter: Is there anything wrong when the woman works?

Śrīla Prabhupāda: There are so many things wrong, but the first thing is, why should some man's wife and child become a burden to the government or the public? First of all answer this. Why should she become a burden?

Reporter: *[No reply]*

Śrīla Prabhupāda: What is your answer?

Reporter: Well, men are burdens to the government, too.

Śrīla Prabhupāda: Do you think, from the social point of view, that this situation of women and fatherless children is a very nice thing?

Reporter: What I'm trying to say is that . . . this may happen to some women . . . I'm talking about women who are not . . .

Śrīla Prabhupāda: This is the general pattern. You cannot say "some." In America I see they are mostly women . . . The woman should be subordinate to the man, so that the man can take charge of the woman. Then the woman is not a problem for the public.

Reporter: Is this true for all women and all men?

Śrīla Prabhupāda: Yes. That is the law of nature. You

take even the dogs—they also take care of their children. The tigers—they take care of their children. So in the human society, if the woman is made pregnant and the man goes away, then she is embarrassed—she has to beg from the government. That is not a very good situation.

Reporter: What about women who do not have children?

Śrīla Prabhupāda: Well, that is another unnatural thing. Sometimes they use contraceptives, or they kill their children—abortion. That is also not very good. These are all sinful activities.

Reporter: Excuse me?

Śrīla Prabhupāda: These are sinful activities—killing the child in the womb by taking shelter of abortion. These are all sinful activities. One has to suffer for them.

Reporter: Is the social unrest in this country caused because . . .

Śrīla Prabhupāda: Because of these things. They do not know that.

"You Are Not the Supreme"

The following conversation between Śrīla Prabhupāda and some of his disciples took place in September of 1975 on an early-morning walk in Vṛndāvana, India.

Śrīla Prabhupāda: Both the living entity and Lord Kṛṣṇa are full of consciousness. The living entity's consciousness is within himself, and Kṛṣṇa's consciousness pervades everywhere. That's the distinction.

Disciple: The Māyāvādīs [impersonalists] say that when we become liberated we will also pervade everywhere. We will merge into Brahman and lose our individual identity.

Śrīla Prabhupāda: That means you will forget everything. Whatever little consciousness you had will be finished.

Disciple: But what we will be forgetting is just illusion anyway.

Śrīla Prabhupāda: If that is liberation, then let me kill you now. You will forget everything—liberation. *[Laughter]*

[A passer-by is singing in Hindi.] This is liberation—he is singing, "O my Lord Kṛṣṇa, when will I surrender unto Your lotus feet?" That is liberation. Just like a child who is fully surrendered to his parents—he is liberated. He has no anxiety. He is confident: "Oh, my parents are here. Whatever they do is all right for me. No one can harm me."

Disciple: The impersonalists say that liberation is getting rid of all misery.
Śrīla Prabhupāda: Yes, if you are full of anxieties, where is your liberation?
Disciple: They say this can be accomplished if we become one with the Supreme.
Śrīla Prabhupāda: Kṛṣṇa is the supreme consciousness. If you lose your consciousness, how do you become one with Him?
Disciple: Well, it's not exactly that we lose our consciousness but that we merge into the supreme consciousness.
Śrīla Prabhupāda: That means you want to become God. But why are you different from God now?
Disciple: It's my *līlā* [pastime].
Śrīla Prabhupāda: But if it's your *līlā*, then why are you undergoing so much austerity to gain liberation?
Disciple: The point is that the supreme consciousness is unembodied, but we are embodied right now. So when we attain supreme consciousness, we will also become unembodied.
Śrīla Prabhupāda: But how have you become embodied if you are the Supreme? What made you embodied? You don't like to be embodied—the body is bringing so much suffering—so you want liberation. But whoever made you embodied—He is the Supreme. You are not the Supreme.
Disciple: I put myself in illusion so that I can enjoy becoming liberated.
Śrīla Prabhupāda: Why would any sane man put himself in a position of being repeatedly kicked by the material nature in the form of birth, old age, disease, and death? What is the enjoyment?
Disciple: Without pain, how can you experience pleasure?

Śrīla Prabhupāda: Then let me kick you, and you can enjoy pleasure when I stop.

Disciple: The idea is that after we experience the suffering of this world, liberation will be very sweet.

Śrīla Prabhupāda: But why is there suffering? If you are supreme, why is there any suffering for you? What is this nonsense—"Suffering is my *līlā*"?

Disciple: It's suffering only for those who don't understand that they are supreme. They are the ones who suffer, but I don't.

Śrīla Prabhupāda: Then you are just like the hogs and dogs. They do not understand that this is suffering. But we can understand. Therefore the Māyāvādīs are *mūḍhas,* fools and rascals, who don't know what suffering is or what enjoyment is. *Mūḍho 'yaṁ nābhijānāti loko mām ajam avyayam.* Kṛṣṇa says, "The fools and rascals don't know that I am Supreme."

Therefore, after many lifetimes of suffering and talking all kinds of nonsense, one who has real knowledge surrenders to Kṛṣṇa (*bahūnāṁ janmanām ante jñānavān māṁ prapadyate*). That is knowledge. When one comes to this awareness—"I have simply suffered, and I have tried to delude myself by a jugglery of words"—then he surrenders to Kṛṣṇa.

Disciple: So the Māyāvāda philosophy is actually the supreme illusion?

Śrīla Prabhupāda: Yes. *Māyāvādi-bhāṣya śunile haya sarva-nāśa:* "One who follows the Māyāvāda philosophy is finished." He's doomed. He will become absorbed in that false philosophy and never be able to accept real philosophy. Māyāvādīs are offenders. Therefore they shall remain perpetually in ignorance and think themselves God. They openly preach, "Why are you thinking that you are sinful? You are God."

Disciple: The Christians have a concept of sin. When

the Māyāvādīs went to America, they told the Christians, "Forget this idea of sin. Whatever you do, it is all right, because you are God."

Śrīla Prabhupāda: The Christian priests did not like the Māyāvāda philosophy. The Māyāvādīs are atheists, more than the Buddhists. The Buddhists do not accept Vedic authority. Therefore they are considered atheists. But the Māyāvādī rascals accept the *Vedas* and preach atheism. So they are more dangerous than the Buddhists. The Buddhists, although they are supposed to be atheists, worship Lord Buddha. He is an incarnation of Kṛṣṇa, so one day they will be delivered. But Māyāvādīs will never be delivered.

Kṛṣṇa assures us in the *Bhagavad-gītā* [18.66]: "Just surrender to Me and I will free you from all dangers." And we accept Kṛṣṇa. That's all. Our method is very easy. The child is trying to walk, but he is unable and he's falling down. The father says, "My dear child, just catch my hand." Then the child is safe.

These Māyāvādīs go against the verdict of God. God says, "The living entities are part and parcel of Me," and the Māyāvādīs say, "I am God." That is their foolishness. If they were equal to God, why does God say, "Surrender to Me"? They are not God. They are simply rascals who are claiming to be equal to God because they do not want to surrender to him.

So this knowledge—that "I must surrender to God"—comes only after many, many births. Then one gives up this foolish word jugglery and attains real liberation in Kṛṣṇa consciousness.

How Work Can Be Worship

The following conversation between Śrīla Prabhupāda and some of his disciples took place in June of 1974 during an early-morning walk in Geneva.

Disciple: What does Kṛṣṇa mean when He says in the *Bhagavad-gītā* that we should be desireless?

Śrīla Prabhupāda: He means that we should desire only to serve Him. Śrī Caitanya Mahāprabhu said, *na dhanaṁ na janaṁ na sundarīṁ kavitāṁ vā jagad-īśa kāmaye:* "I don't want wealth. I don't want followers. I don't want beautiful women." Then what does He want? "I want to serve Kṛṣṇa." It is not that He says, "I don't want this, I don't want that. Let Me become zero." No.

Disciple: The nondevotee also says he knows what he wants, but he says, "I can achieve the same good results without Kṛṣṇa."

Śrīla Prabhupāda: Then he is a fool, because he does not know what good results really are. Today he is struggling very hard for one "good result," but tomorrow he'll desire something else, because he must undergo a change of body when he dies. Sometimes he's taking the body of a dog and desiring one "good result," and sometimes he's taking the body of a demigod and desiring another "good result." *Bhramatām upary adhaḥ:* he's wandering up and down the universe, just like . . . what is that?

Disciple: A Ferris wheel.

Śrīla Prabhupāda: Yes. Sometimes he is rising to an elevated position, and then again he must come down and take the body of a dog or hog. This is going on.

brahmāṇḍa bhramite kona bhāgyavān jīva
guru-kṛṣṇa-prasāde pāya bhakti-latā-bīja

"After wandering up and down the universe for many lifetimes, one who is very fortunate comes to devotional life by the mercy of the spiritual master and Kṛṣṇa." [*Caitanya-caritāmṛta, Madhya* 19.151]

Disciple: Well, the nondevotee will say, "We are also doing good service. You are distributing food, and we are also distributing food. You are opening schools, and we are also opening schools."

Śrīla Prabhupāda: Yes, but we are opening schools that teach Kṛṣṇa consciousness, while your schools are teaching illusion. The problem is that the rascals cannot understand the difference between *bhakti* [devotional service] and *karma* [material activity]. *Bhakti* looks like *karma,* but it's not *karma.* In *bhakti* we also work, but for Kṛṣṇa's sake. That is the difference.

For example, Arjuna fought in the Battle of Kurukṣetra, but because he fought for Kṛṣṇa he is accepted as a great devotee. Kṛṣṇa told him, *bhakto 'si me . . . priyo 'si me:* "Arjuna, you are My dear devotee." What did Arjuna do? He fought, that's all. But he fought for Kṛṣṇa. That is the secret. He did not change his fighting capacity as a warrior, but he changed his mentality. At first he was thinking, "Why shall I kill my kinsmen? Let me leave the battlefield and go to the forest and become a mendicant." But Kṛṣṇa wanted him to fight, so at last he surrendered and did it as a service for Kṛṣṇa. Not for his own sense gratification, but for Kṛṣṇa's sense gratification.

Disciple: So sense gratification is there even in devotional service?

Śrīla Prabhupāda: Yes. A *karmī* [materialist] works for his own sense gratification, and a *bhakta* works for Kṛṣṇa's sense gratification. That is the difference between a nondevotee and a devotee. Sense gratification is there in either case, but when you work for your personal sense gratification it is *karma*, and when you work for Kṛṣṇa's sense gratification it is *bhakti. Bhakti* and *karma* look similar, but the quality is different.

Another example is the behaviour of the *gopīs* [Kṛṣṇa's cowherd girlfriends]. Kṛṣṇa was a beautiful boy and the *gopīs* were attracted to Him. They wanted Him as their lover, and they went out from their homes in the middle of the night to dance with Him. So it appears that they acted sinfully—but they did not, because the centre was Kṛṣṇa. Therefore Caitanya Mahāprabhu recommends, *ramyā kācid upāsanā vrajavadhūvargeṇa yā kalpitā:* "There is no better mode of worshipping Kṛṣṇa than that practised by the *gopīs.*"

But the rascals think, "Oh, this is very good. Kṛṣṇa danced in the middle of the night with other men's wives, so let us also gather some girls and dance, and we will also enjoy like Kṛṣṇa." This is a gross misunderstanding of Kṛṣṇa's pastimes with the *gopīs.* To prevent this misunderstanding, Śrīla Vyāsadeva [the author of *Śrīmad-Bhāgavatam*] has devoted nine cantos of the *Bhāgavatam* to describing Kṛṣṇa's position as the Supreme Personality of Godhead. Then he gives a description of Kṛṣṇa's behaviour with the *gopīs.* But the rascals jump immediately to the Tenth Canto, to Kṛṣṇa's dealings with the *gopīs.* In this way they become *sahajiyās* [imitators of Kṛṣṇa].

Disciple: Will such persons experience a change of heart, since they're somehow or other associating with Kṛṣṇa?

Śrīla Prabhupāda: No. Kaṁsa also associated with Kṛṣṇa—but as an enemy. That is not *bhakti. Bhakti* must be *ānukūlyena kṛṣṇānu-śīlanaṁ:* favourable devotional service. One should not imitate Kṛṣṇa or try to kill Him. That is also Kṛṣṇa consciousness, but it is not favourable and therefore is not *bhakti*. Still, the enemies of Kṛṣṇa get salvation, because they have somehow or other thought of Kṛṣṇa. They get impersonal liberation, but they are not allowed to enter into the pastimes of Kṛṣṇa in the spiritual world. That benediction is reserved for those who practice pure loving devotion to Kṛṣṇa.

On Christians, Communists, and Cow-killers

The following conversation between Śrīla Prabhupāda and some of his disciples took place during an early-morning walk in March of 1975 in Dallas.

Śrīla Prabhupāda: The Christians say, "We can commit all kinds of sin, but Christ will take our sins on himself. He has taken a contract." Do they not say something like that?

Disciple: Yes.

Śrīla Prabhupāda: Poor Christ has to suffer for all their sinful activities. "He wanted to save us from sin," they say, "so he gave us an injunction that we don't have to care whether we sin or not." This is hypocrisy.

In Melbourne I was invited by some priests to speak. They asked me, "Why do you think the Christian religion is dwindling? What have we done?" So I replied, "What have you not done? You claim that you are followers of Jesus Christ, yet you are performing all kinds of sinful activities. Therefore you will soon have to close down this hypocrisy." They were not very much pleased with that answer.

"What have we done?" they ask. They have done so many sinful things, but they do not admit they are sinful. This is hypocrisy. In the Ten Commandments the Bible clearly says, "Thou shalt not kill." But they'll not obey. That is sinful.

Wilful sinners. If one acts sinfully out of ignorance

there may be some concession, but they are knowingly sinful. They know that killing cows is sinful, yet still they are doing it.

Disciple: Most Christians don't think it's a sin to eat meat, Śrīla Prabhupāda.

Śrīla Prabhupāda: That means the priests are rascals for misinterpreting the Bible. This hypocrisy is going on in the name of religion. But how long can those who preach such ideas cheat others? You can cheat all people sometimes, and you can cheat some people all of the time, but you can't cheat all people all of the time.

Disciple: The communists also argue that the Christian religion is hypocrisy. They say it is "the opium of the people." So they want to abolish it.

Śrīla Prabhupāda: The communists have had a bad experience with the Christian religion, and they have no information that there is a *need* of religion. So they want to abolish all religion.

Disciple: The communists say that the problems of the world are so great that unless people give allegiance to a world government, the problems cannot be solved.

Śrīla Prabhupāda: We also say that. Kṛṣṇa is the Supreme Lord; take shelter of Him and all problems will be solved. That we are also teaching.

Disciple: But the communists have missed the point that Kṛṣṇa must be recognized as the Supreme Lord.

Śrīla Prabhupāda: *Ekale īśvara kṛṣṇa, āra saba bhṛtya:* "The only master is Kṛṣṇa. Everyone else is His servant." This is the central principle of the *Bhagavad-gītā.* Accept this principle and everything will be all right, immediately.

If you study the *Bhagavad-gītā,* you won't find any word that you can refute or that is not good for you. The whole *Bhagavad-gītā* is practical—very congenial for human civilisation. First Kṛṣṇa teaches that you must learn who you are. You are not the body. You are a spirit soul within the body. Who knows this? This is the first lesson Kṛṣṇa teaches in the *Bhagavad-gītā.* As soon as you understand that you are not the body but that you are *within* the body, you understand what spirit is. Then your spiritual knowledge advances further. But the rascals do not know what spirit is. So they have no spiritual knowledge.

Disciple: They think cows have no spirit.

Śrīla Prabhupāda: How can they say there is no spirit in cows? You have spirit. Your body is moving. You are working. You are eating. You are talking. And as soon as the spirit soul is gone from your body, the body becomes dead matter. The hands and legs will still be there, but they will not work, because the spirit soul is gone.

So, what is the difference between the cow's body and your body? Come to human reasoning. Is there any essential difference between your body and a cow's body?

Disciple: No. But now they are saying that human beings also have no soul. They say that since the cow has no soul, we can eat the cow, and since human beings have no soul . . .

Śrīla Prabhupāda: . . . you can kill the baby in the womb. Advancement of ignorance is accepted as advancement of civilisation. Why? Because there is no spiritual knowledge.

[*Śrīla Prabhupāda and his disciples pass a man playing golf.*]

Disciple: That man thinks he has retired from working hard, but he's still working hard just to put a ball in a hole.

Śrīla Prabhupāda: What else can he do? He doesn't know that there is another engagement: spiritual life. That is his ignorance.

When there was an electricity failure in New York, the statistics showed that more women became pregnant. What else could people do in the darkness? "Let us have sex." That's all. Without spiritual knowledge, human beings become just like animals.

On Sex and Suffering

The following conversation between Śrīla Prabhupāda and some of his disciples took place on an early-morning walk in January of 1974 at Venice Beach, California.

Disciple: Śrīla Prabhupāda, here in California the divorce rate is nearly fifty percent. Why do you think that is so?

Śrīla Prabhupāda: In India there is a saying that he who is married laments and he who is not married also laments. The married man laments, "Why did I marry? I could have remained free." And he who is not married laments, "Oh, why didn't I accept a wife? I would have been happy." [*Laughter*]

By sex one begets a child, and as soon as there is a child there is suffering. The child suffers, and the parents also suffer to take care of him. But again they have another child. Therefore it is said in *Śrīmad-Bhāgavatam* [7.9.45], *tṛpyanti neha kṛpaṇā bahu-duḥkha-bhājaḥ.* In connection with this child-producing there is so much difficulty and trouble, but although one *knows* that, one again does the same thing.

Sex is the main happiness in this material world. That is the main happiness, and it is very abominable. What is this happiness? *Kaṇḍūyanena karayor iva duḥkha-duḥkham.* It is like the rubbing of two hands together to relieve an itch. Sex produces so many bad results, but still one is not satisfied. Now there are contraceptives, abortion—so many things. Māyā [illusion] is so strong; she says, "Yes, do this and be implicated."

Therefore the *Bhāgavatam* says, *kaṇḍūtivan manasijaṁ viṣaheta dhīraḥ*. A man who is *dhīra,* sober and sane, tolerates this itching sensation of sex desire. One who can tolerate the itching sensation saves so much trouble, but one who cannot is immediately implicated. Whether illicit or legitimate, sex is trouble.

Disciple: Śrīla Prabhupāda, this is the first time we've walked this way. Everything looks different and new.

Śrīla Prabhupāda: [*Laughs*] This is material life. We are wandering sometimes this way, sometimes that way, and we are thinking, "Oh, this is new." *Brahmāṇḍa bhramite:* we are wandering all over the universe trying to find out something new. But nothing is new: everything is old.

When a man becomes old, he generally thinks, "Oh, this life is so troublesome." So he is allowed to change to a new body, a child's body. The child is taken care of, and he thinks, "Now I've got such a comfortable life." But again he becomes old and disgusted. So, Kṛṣṇa is so kind: "All right," He says, "change your body." This is *punaḥ punaś carvita-carvaṇānām,* chewing the chewed. Kṛṣṇa gives the living entity many facilities: "All right, become a tree. All right, become a serpent. All right, become a demigod. All right, become a king. All right, become a cobbler. Go to the heavenly planets. Go to the hellish planets." There are so many varieties of life, but in all of them the living entity is packed up in this material world. He's looking for freedom, but he does not know that freedom is available only under the shelter of Kṛṣṇa. That he will not accept.

Seeing the suffering in this material world, the Māyāvādīs [impersonalists] want to make life variety-less (*nirviśeṣa*) and the Buddhists want to make it zero (*śūnya*). But neither proposition is possible. You may remain variety-less for some time, but again you will want varieties. Big, big *sannyāsīs* [renunciants] preach so much about *brahma satyaṁ jagan mithyā* ["The impersonal Absolute is true; this universe is false"], but again they come down from Brahman to do political and social work. They cannot remain in Brahman for long, so they have to accept this material variety, because variety is the mother of enjoyment. Therefore, our proposition is this: Come to the real variety, Kṛṣṇa consciousness. Then your life will be successful.

Disciple: Most people are trying to enjoy so much in this life that they don't even think about the next life.

Śrīla Prabhupāda: They do not know what the next life is, so they make it zero. They say, "There is no next life," and in that way they are satisfied. When a rabbit sees some danger it closes its eyes and thinks there is no danger. These rascals are like that. It is all ignorance.

Disciple: There is a philosophy called stoicism, which says that since life is meant for suffering, one should just become very sturdy and suffer a great deal.

Śrīla Prabhupāda: So, their idea is that one who can suffer without any protest, he is a first-class man. Believing in such a philosophy means that one does not know how to stop suffering.

One class of philosophers says that suffering cannot be dismissed and therefore we must be strong to tolerate it. And another class of philosophers says that since life is full of suffering, we should make life zero. But neither class has any information that there is real life where there is no suffering. That is Kṛṣṇa consciousness. There is life, but no suffering. *Ānandamayo 'bhyāsāt:* simply bliss. Dancing, eating, and chanting, with no suffering. Would anybody refuse that? Is there any such fool?

Disciple: People deny that such a life exists.

Śrīla Prabhupāda: But suppose there is such a life, where you can simply dance, eat, and live happily for eternity. Would you not like to accept it?

Disciple: Anyone would like to accept it. But people think it doesn't exist.

Śrīla Prabhupāda: So our first proposition should be that there is a life like this: only happiness with no suffering. Everyone will say, "Yes, I would like it." They will accept it. Unfortunately, because people have been cheated again and again, they think that this is another cheating. Therefore, preaching Kṛṣṇa consciousness means to convince people that there is a life full of happiness, with no suffering,

Disciple: What will convince them that we are not cheating also?

Śrīla Prabhupāda: Invite them to come to our temple and see our devotees. We are chanting, dancing, and eating nicely. This is practical proof.

Disciple: But doesn't one have to be purified before one can realise these things?

Śrīla Prabhupāda: No. We say, "Come and chant Hare Kṛṣṇa with us; you'll become purified. We don't want anything from you. We shall give you food; we shall give you everything. Simply come and chant with us." This is our message.

On Technology and Unemployment

This exchange between Śrīla Prabhupāda and one of his disciples took place in Geneva in June of 1974.

Disciple: In a recent speech a politician in India said that eighty percent of the Indian people live in rural villages. His proposal was to increase the technology on the farms. Instead of people having to harvest the wheat by hand, they would have motorised harvesters, and instead of having to use bullocks to pull the plough, they'd use a tractor.

Śrīla Prabhupāda: In India many men are already unemployed, so to introduce more machinery there is a not a very good proposal. One hundred men's work can be done by one man working a machine. But why should there be so many men unemployed? Why not engage one hundred men instead of one? Here in the West, also, there is much unemployment. Because in your Western countries everything is done by machine, you are creating many hippies, frustrated young people with nothing to do. That is another kind of unemployment. So in many cases machines create unemployment.

Everyone should be employed; otherwise there will be trouble. "An idle brain is a devil's workshop." When there are so many people without any engagement, why should we introduce machinery to create more unemployment? The best policy is that nobody should be unemployed; everyone should be busy.

Disciple: But someone might argue, "The machine is freeing us from so much time-consuming labour."

Śrīla Prabhupāda: Free for what? For drinking and doing all kinds of nonsense. What is the meaning of this freedom? If you make people free to cultivate Kṛṣṇa consciousness, that is another thing. Of course, when someone comes to our Kṛṣṇa consciousness movement, he should also be fully engaged. This movement is not meant for eating and sleeping, but for working for Kṛṣṇa. So whether here in Kṛṣṇa consciousness or there in the outer society, the policy should be that everyone should be employed and busy. Then there will be a good civilisation.

In the Vedic civilisation, it was the duty of the head of society to see that everyone was working, either as a *brāhmaṇa* [an intellectual or teacher], a *kṣatriya* [a military or political leader] a *vaiśya* [a farmer or merchant], or a *śūdra* [a labourer]. Everyone must work; then there will be peace. At the present moment we can see that on account of so much technology, there are unemployment and many lazy fellows. The hippies are lazy, that's all. They don't want to do anything.

Disciple: Another argument might be that with technology we can work so much better, so much more efficiently, so the productivity of those who do work goes way up.

Śrīla Prabhupāda: Better that more men be employed doing the work less efficiently. In the *Bhagavad-gītā* [18.48] Kṛṣṇa says:

saha-jaṁ karma kaunteya sa-doṣam api na tyajet
sarvārambhā hi doṣeṇa dhūmenāgnir ivāvṛtāḥ

"Every endeavour is covered by some sort of fault, just as fire is covered by smoke. Therefore one should not give up the work which is born of his nature, O son of Kuntī, even if such work is full of fault." And a Hindi proverb says, "*Bekārī se begārī acchī hai.*" *Bekārī* means "without employment." And *begārī* means "to work without salary." In India, we have seen many villagers come and request a shopkeeper, or any gentleman, "Please, give me some work. I don't want a salary. If you like, you can give me something to eat. Otherwise, I don't even want that." So, what gentleman, if you work at his place, will not give you something to eat? Immediately the worker gets some occupation, along with food and shelter. Then, when he's working, if the gentleman sees that he's working very nicely, he will say, "All right, take some salary." Therefore it is better to work without any remuneration than to remain lazy, without any work. That is a very dangerous position. But in the modern civilisation, on account of too many machines, there are so many unemployed people, and so many lazies also. It is not good.

Disciple: Most people would say these ideas are very old-fashioned. They'd rather have their technology, even if it creates a high unemployment rate, because they see it as a means of freedom from drudgery, and also as a means of freedom to enjoy television, movies, automobiles . . .

Śrīla Prabhupāda: Technology is not freedom. Rather, it is a freeway to hell. It is not freedom. Everyone should be engaged in work according to his ability. If you have good intelligence, you may do the work of a *brāhmaṇa*—studying scriptures and writing books, giving knowledge to others. That is the *brāhmaṇa's* work. You don't have to bother about your subsistence. The society will supply it. In the Vedic civilisation *brāhmaṇas* did not work for a salary. They were busy studying the Vedic literature and teaching others, and the society gave them food.

As for the *kṣatriyas,* they must give protection to the other members of society. There will be danger, there will be attack, and the *kṣatriyas* should protect the people. For that purpose they may levy taxes. Then, those who are less intelligent than the *kṣatriyas* are the *vaiśyas,* the mercantile community, who engage in producing food and giving protection to the cows. These things are required. And finally there are the *śūdras,* who help the three higher classes.

This is the natural division of society, and it is very good, because it was created by Kṛṣṇa Himself (*cātur-varṇyaṁ mayā sṛṣṭaṁ*). Everyone is employed. The intelligent class is employed, the martial class is employed, the mercantile class is employed, and the rest, the *śūdras,* are also employed. There is no need to form political parties and fight. In Vedic times there was no such thing. The king was the supervisor who saw that everyone was engaged in his respective duty. So people had no time to form false political parties and make agitation and fight one another. There was no such chance.

But the beginning of everything is to understand, "I am not this body," and this is stressed again and again by Kṛṣṇa in the *Bhagavad-gītā.*

On Science and Belief

The following conversation between Śrīla Prabhupāda and one of his disciples was recorded during an early-morning walk in Perth, Australia, in May of 1975.

Disciple: *[Taking the part of a materialistic scientist]* Why do you call Kṛṣṇa consciousness a science? It seems like it's only a belief.

Śrīla Prabhupāda: Your so-called science is also belief. If you call your way science, then our way is also science.

Disciple: But with our science we can prove our beliefs.

Śrīla Prabhupāda: Then prove that chemicals make life. Your belief is that life is made from chemicals. So prove it; then it is science. But you cannot prove it; therefore it remains a belief.

Disciple: Well, you believe in the soul, but you can't prove that it exists. Since we cannot see the soul, we have to conclude that life comes from matter.

Śrīla Prabhupāda: You cannot see the soul with your gross senses, but it can be perceived. Consciousness can be perceived, and consciousness is the symptom of the soul. But if, as you say, life comes from matter, then you must demonstrate it by supplying the missing chemicals to make a dead body live again. This is my challenge.

Disciple: It will require some time to find the right chemicals.

Śrīla Prabhupāda: That means you are talking nonsense. Your belief is that life comes from chemicals, but you cannot prove it. Therefore, you prove yourself to be a rascal.

Disciple: But you accept the *Bhagavad-gītā* on faith. How is that scientific? It's only your belief, isn't that correct?
Śrīla Prabhupāda: Why isn't it scientific? The *Bhagavad-gītā* says, *annād bhavanti bhūtāni parjanyād anna-sambhavaḥ:* "All living entities subsist by eating sufficient food grains, and grains are produced from rain." Is that belief?
Disciple: That must be true.
Śrīla Prabhupāda: Similarly, everything in the *Bhagavad-gītā* is true. If you think about it carefully, you will find it is all true. In the *Bhagavad-gītā* Kṛṣṇa says that in society there must be an intelligent class of men, the *brāhmaṇas,* who know the soul and God. That is civilised man. But where is such a class of men in today's society?
Disciple: There are many rabbis, priests, and ministers.
Śrīla Prabhupāda: But what do they know about God? Just try to see this one point clearly. There is a supreme authority. You are not independent; therefore, you have to accept that a supreme authority exists. But you do not know who that supreme authority is. So if you do not know the supreme authority, what is the value of your knowledge?

Suppose a man does not know about the government of his country. What kind of man is he? He is simply a third-class man, a rascal. A civilised man knows about his country's government. Similarly, there is a government of the whole universe, but if you do not know it, you are a third-class, uncivilised man. Therefore, Lord Kṛṣṇa teaches in the *Bhagavad-gītā* that in human society there must be an intelligent class of men, who know God and who understand the whole universal management—how it is running under the order of God. We Kṛṣṇa conscious devotees know these things. Therefore we are civilised.

Disciple: But the *Bhagavad-gītā* was written five thousand years ago, so it doesn't pertain to today.
Śrīla Prabhupāda: The *Bhagavad-gītā* was not written five thousand years ago: it was already there. It has always existed. Do you study the *Bhagavad-gītā?*
Disciple: Yes.
Śrīla Prabhupāda: Then where do you find in the *Bhagavad-gītā* that it was written five thousand years ago? It was first spoken more than 120 million years ago. Kṛṣṇa says *imaṁ vivasvate yogaṁ proktavān aham avyayam:* "I spoke this science to Vivasvān more than 120 million years ago." You do not know this? What kind of reader of the *Bhagavad-gītā* are you? The *Bhagavad-gītā* is *avyayam*—it is eternally existing. So how can you say it was written five thousand years ago?
[Śrīla Prabhupāda points to the rising sun with his cane.]

Here we see the sun is just rising. But it is always there, in space. The *Bhagavad-gītā* is like that: it is eternal truth. When the sun is rising we don't say it is just now coming into existence. It is always there, but we can't see it until it rises. Men used to think that at night the sun would die and in the morning a new sun was created. They also used to believe the earth was flat. This is your scientific knowledge: every day a new opinion.
Disciple: This means that we are discovering the truth.
Śrīla Prabhupāda: No. It means you do not know what the truth is. You are only speculating. Now you accept something as true, but after a few days you say it is not true. And you call this science!
Disciple: Yes, you're right. Many of the scientific textbooks that were written just a few years ago are outdated now.
Śrīla Prabhupāda: And the scientific books you are now using will be useless in a few years. This is your science.

Disciple: But at least what we know now is more true than what we knew before, and if we keep trying we will know more.

Śrīla Prabhupāda: This means you are always in ignorance. But the *Bhagavad-gītā* is not like that. Kṛṣṇa says to Arjuna, "I first instructed this science 120 million years ago, and today I am teaching you the same thing." That is scientific knowledge. The truth is always the same, but you scientists are always changing—"discovering the truth," you call it. That means you do not know what truth is.

Disciple: *[As himself]* The problem is, everyone is a cheater. Everyone is speculating and presenting his own conclusions as the truth.

Śrīla Prabhupāda: Yes. Therefore we have accepted Kṛṣṇa, the person who does not cheat. And since I am presenting only what Kṛṣṇa has said, I am also not a cheater. That is the difference between us and the scientists.

On Education and "The Good Life"

The following exchange between Śrīla Prabhupāda, the mother of a new devotee, and a Jesuit priest took place in July of 1973 at the Rādhā-Kṛṣṇa temple, London.

Śrīla Prabhupāda: *[To the mother]* According to our Vedic understanding, there are four pillars of sinful life: illicit sex, unnecessary killing of animals, intoxication, and gambling. Our students have been trained to give these up. And as you can see from your son, they are happy and satisfied by eating nice foods made from vegetables and milk and by chanting Hare Kṛṣṇa, the holy name of God.

Mother: I see he's happy. But, you know, he came from a very happy home, so he should be happy, shouldn't he?

Śrīla Prabhupāda: Yes. But now he's still happier. He was happy, but now he's happier.

Mother: I'm happy for Michael's happiness, but I'm very disappointed that he's not continuing his university education.

Śrīla Prabhupāda: Our Kṛṣṇa consciousness movement is not depriving people of their education. We say, "Go on with your university education, but side by side become competent to know God and to love Him. Then your life is perfect."

But in any case, what is the purpose of education? Our Vedic culture teaches that the culmination of education is to understand God. That is education.

Otherwise, the education for learning how to eat nicely, how to sleep nicely, how to have sex and defend nicely—this education is there even among the animals. The animals also know how to eat, how to sleep, how to have sex, and how to defend. These four branches of education are not sufficient for human beings. A human being must know how to love God: that is perfection.

Mother: Yes. I agree with you completely. I could mention a lot of brilliant men in science who are still very close to God. Where would we be without our scientists, without our doctors . . .

Śrīla Prabhupāda: But simply to become a doctor in medical science will not save one. Unfortunately, most doctors do not believe in the next life.

Mother: Oh, yes, they do. I know a doctor who comes to church every Sunday—and Michael knows him too. He believes in the next life; he's a *very good* man.

Śrīla Prabhupāda: Generally people in the West who believe in the next life do not believe in it very seriously. If they actually believed in the next life, they would be more concerned about what *kind* of next life they were going to have. There are 8,400,000 forms of life. The trees are a form of life, the cats and dogs are also forms of life, and the worm in the stool is also a form of life. So, all together there are 8,400,000 species. Since we are going to have a next life, since we have to leave our present body and take another body, our main concern should be what kind of body we are going to get next. But where is that university which educates its students to prepare for the next life?

Priest: Catholic universities all over the world are doing that, and that's our main purpose: to teach the young man or the young girl success in this world but, above all, success in the next, which means union with God for eternity. That's top priority.

Śrīla Prabhupāda: So, how can we know what kind of body we are going to have in our next life?
Priest: All I know is that there's no annihilation. I'm going to be joined with God.
Mother: We're going to be joined with Almighty God, that's all. We're going to Almighty God when we die. We don't have to worry.
Śrīla Prabhupāda: But what is the qualification for going to God? Does everyone go to God?
Mother and Priest: Yes. Yes.
Priest: Everybody who believes in God and who leads a good life and does his best in this world . . .
Śrīla Prabhupāda: Then the next question is, What is the good life?
Priest: Obeying the commandments of God.
Śrīla Prabhupāda: One commandment is, Thou shalt not kill. So if somebody kills innocent animals and eats them, is he leading the good life?
Priest: Father, you're being a bit unfair. *Thou shalt not kill* means "Thou shalt not unnecessarily take away life." How would we be able to live if we didn't eat meat?
Śrīla Prabhupāda: How are we living? We are eating nice foods prepared from vegetables, grains, fruits, and milk. We don't need meat.
Priest: Look at it this way. You just said a few minutes ago that there are eight million or so different kinds of life. Would you agree that the potato, the cabbage, and other vegetables also have life?
Śrīla Prabhupāda: Yes.
Priest: So when you boil those vegetables, you're taking away their life.
Śrīla Prabhupāda: What is your philosophy—that killing a potato and killing an innocent animal are equal?
Priest: You said, "Thou shalt not kill," but you kill the potato.

Śrīla Prabhupāda: We all have to live by eating other living entities: *jīvo jīvasya jīvanam.* But eating a potato and eating some animal are not the same. Do you think they are equal?

Priest: Yes.

Śrīla Prabhupāda: Then why don't you kill a child and eat it?

Priest: I wouldn't for a second think of killing a child.

Śrīla Prabhupāda: But animals and children are alike in that they both are helpless and ignorant. Because a child is ignorant, that does not mean we can kill him. Similarly, although animals may be ignorant or unintelligent, we should not kill them unnecessarily. A reasonable man, a religious man, should discriminate. He should think, "If I can get my food from vegetables, fruits, and milk, why should I kill and eat animals?" Besides, when you get a fruit from a tree, there is no killing. Similarly, when we take milk from a cow, we don't kill the cow. So, if we can live in such a way without killing, why should we kill animals?

Priest: Would you say that because I eat meat and bacon and so on—does that make me sinful? If I didn't eat those, I would be less sinful?

Śrīla Prabhupāda: Yes.

Priest: So if I give up eating meat and bacon and sausages, I would become a different person?

Śrīla Prabhupāda: You would become purified.

Priest: That's very interesting.

Śrīla Prabhupāda: Animal-killers cannot understand God. I have seen this; it is a fact. They do not have the brain to understand God.

On Abortion and "Rabbit Philosophy"

The following conversation between Śrīla Prabhupāda and some of his disciples took place on an early-morning walk in December of 1973 at Venice Beach, California.

Disciple: Śrīla Prabhupāda, sometimes we argue that although the laws of nature are very powerful, we can overcome such things as disease and death if we surrender to Lord Kṛṣṇa, since He is controlling nature. But sceptics say we can gradually come to control the laws of nature on our own, without God.

Śrīla Prabhupāda: No, we are forced to accept the laws of nature. How can anyone say he has conquered the laws of nature?

Disciple: Well, the doctors and biologists have conquered so many diseases.

Śrīla Prabhupāda: But people are still becoming diseased. How have the doctors stopped disease?

Disciple: In Africa and India, for instance, they are inoculating everyone against smallpox, and they've saved many thousands of children from dying.

Śrīla Prabhupāda: But the children will grow up and get old and die eventually in any case. So death has not been stopped. And besides, why do they bother about these children? They don't want overpopulation, so logically the doctors should let them die. But the doctors are illogical. On one side they want to check the death of children, and on the other side they recommend the use of contraceptives and kill the children in the womb by abortion. Why? Why are they killing? To check the increase in population. Then when children are dying in another part of the world, why are they anxious to save them?

Disciple: Once the child is born, they want to save him. But when the child is still in the womb they feel they can kill him. They say he is not yet a human being.

Śrīla Prabhupāda: But the child is already born as soon as a woman becomes pregnant. Pregnancy *means* the child is already born. How can they say there is no child? What is this nonsense? When a woman is pregnant, why do we say she is "with child"? This means the child is already born. Therefore, I say this abortion business is simply rascaldom.

Disciple: Well, they've rationalised it.

Śrīla Prabhupāda: How?

Disciple: Sometimes they say they're just doing what they feel is best. And of course they deny that there's any such thing as *karma* to punish them later. It seems like they have a kind of "rabbit philosophy." When a rabbit closes his eyes so he doesn't see the wolf bearing down on him, he may actually think he's safe.

Śrīla Prabhupāda: So, the abortionists believe in rabbit philosophy. It is not a man's philosophy. It is rabbit's philosophy, frog's philosophy, ass's philosophy. And they have been described in *Śrīmad-Bhāgavatam* [2.3.19]: *śva-viḍ-varāhoṣṭra-kharaiḥ saṁstutaḥ puruṣaḥ paśuḥ.* The leaders, who often support abortion, are rascals, and they're glorified by another set of rascals and fools—the people in general. Because the whole population is made up of rascals, they elect a rascal as their leader. Then, being dissatisfied, they throw the first rascal out of office and elect another rascal. This is called *punaḥ punaś carvita-carvaṇānām:* chewing the chewed.

The people do not know whom to elect. Therefore they have to be educated to choose a leader who is God conscious, who is actually fit to be a leader. Then they will be happy. Otherwise, they will go on electing one rascal and rejecting him, electing another rascal and rejecting *him,* and so on.

In America there is a slogan: "In God we trust." We simply say that the standard for a leader should be that he knows who God is and that he trusts in Him. And if people actually want to know who God is, they can read the *Bhagavad-gītā.* They should read it with intelligence and try to understand, and then for further progress they may study *Śrīmad-Bhāgavatam.* It is not that we are theorising. We are taking our information about God from authorised books.

Disciple: In our leaflet about politics, we list the qualifications of a leader. First we say he must follow the four regulative principles: no meat-eating, no illicit sex, no gambling, and no indulging in intoxicants. And the one positive injunction we give is that the leader chant the holy name of the Lord. But someone might argue that these requirements violate the constitutional principle of separation of Church and State.

Śrīla Prabhupāda: If you believe in God, why should you have any objection to chanting the holy name of God? If you say "In God we trust," then you must know the name of God and the address of God. Then you can actually trust Him. And if you don't know these things, then learn them from us. We are giving you God's name, address, qualities—everything. And if you say there is no God, then what is the meaning of "In God we trust"?

Disciple: They have made propaganda to separate Church and State, but they've also separated God and country.

Śrīla Prabhupāda: Those who are making this propaganda do not understand what God is. God cannot be separated from anything, because everything is God (*mayā tatam idaṁ sarvaṁ*). If they study the *Bhagavad-gītā* they will understand that God is present everywhere. It is not possible to separate anything from Him. Just as your consciousness is present in every part of your body, so the supreme consciousness, God, is present everywhere in the universe. Kṛṣṇa says, *vedāhaṁ samatītāni:* "I know everything that has happened." Unless He is everywhere, how can He know everything? What do you say?

Disciple: This is logical, Śrīla Prabhupāda.

Śrīla Prabhupāda: How can you separate God from the government? You may reject any so-called church or any so-called religion that agrees, "Yes, God and the state should be separate." And that is God's instruction—that we reject such so-called religions. *Sarva-dharmān parityajya mām ekaṁ śaraṇaṁ vraja:* "Give up all kinds of so-called religion and simply surrender to Me," Kṛṣṇa says in the *Bhagavad-gītā* [18.66]. People may say they believe in God, but you can know they are ignorant of what God is when they try to separate God from government.

On "Might Makes Right"

This conversation between Śrīla Prabhupāda and one of his disciples took place in Paris in June of 1974.

Disciple: Last night in your lecture you made the analogy that if people don't follow God's laws, they'll be punished by God, just as they're punished for disobeying the state laws. So the young people thought you must be a fascist.

Śrīla Prabhupāda: But this is actually happening all over the world. How can they deny it? Government today means "Might makes right." Somehow you take power, and then you are right. It is a question of which group gets the power:

Disciple: But they want to give the power to the people.

Śrīla Prabhupāda: How will it be possible? There are so many people and so many different opinions—you have your people, and someone else has his people. As soon as you want to give the power to your people, the others will oppose. This is human nature; you cannot change it. They're thinking that the power should be given to the people, but there are many other people who will disagree. This is the nature of the material world: everyone is envious of everyone else. But these rascals don't have the intelligence to understand this. In India there was Gandhi—a gentleman, a very nice politician—but he was killed. So you cannot stop this. It is the nature of the material world—everyone is envious of others. You'll never be able to find a group of materialistic men who are perfect. So why do they say, "Give the power to the people"? They are simply rascals.

Therefore, *Śrīmad-Bhāgavatam* says, *paramo nirmat-sarāṇāṁ satām:* Kṛṣṇa consciousness is for the perfect, nonenvious person. Those who are not Kṛṣṇa conscious must be envious. Everywhere you'll find competition. Kṛṣṇa had enemies. Jesus Christ had enemies, or else why was he crucified? He had no fault; he was preaching God consciousness. Yet he was crucified. This is the material world. Even though one is perfect, still he'll have enemies. How can you stop it? They say, "Give the power to the people," but as soon as there is one good group of people governing, another group will stand against it. They will say, "Give the power to us." So where is your perfection? This is not perfection. Therefore, we have to give up all connection with this material world—that is perfection.

Disciple: But how can you avoid anarchy and have good government if you give up all connection with this world?

Śrīla Prabhupāda: Yes, this is the point: you have to follow the perfect authority.

Disciple: And this was their contention: you advocate following a superior authority.

Śrīla Prabhupāda: If you want a perfect society, you must follow the perfect authority. You cannot find perfection through mundane politics. You have to follow the real, recognized authorities: the perfect, liberated souls. This was the system in the Vedic culture. The authority was Lord Kṛṣṇa and the Vedic literature, and society was directed by Manu [the forefather and lawgiver of mankind] and the *Manu-saṁhitā. Mahājano yena gataḥ sa panthāḥ:* to attain perfection, we must follow the *mahājanas*—perfect, self-realised authorities.

Disciple: But these young people said even spiritual authorities are imperfect.

Śrīla Prabhupāda: They may say that, but why should we accept their opinion—the opinion of imperfect rascals? Their only idea of authority is "Might makes right." For instance, that group yesterday was advocating "Power to the people." So they have got some might, and they are pressuring, "You must accept this idea." And this is going on all over the world—"Might makes right." All the rascals are fighting with one another, and the one who is a little mightier becomes prominent. That's all.

Disciple: They say this is always the case—with any authority, it's just some leader who's pushed himself forward. So they've rejected all authorities.

Śrīla Prabhupāda: Yes, because all their so-called authorities have been imperfect. But there is a perfect authority also: Kṛṣṇa, the Supreme Personality of Godhead. And any authority who follows and teaches according to the instructions of Kṛṣṇa is also perfect. That is authority.

We Kṛṣṇa conscious devotees are exactly following the authority of Kṛṣṇa. In presenting Kṛṣṇa consciousness, we are simply presenting the words of Kṛṣṇa and trying to convince people, "Here is the real authority; if you follow you'll be happy." Kṛṣṇa says, "You surrender unto Me." And we are saying, "Surrender to Kṛṣṇa." We know that Kṛṣṇa is perfect and that to surrender unto Him is perfection. And whenever we speak, we always quote Kṛṣṇa and Kṛṣṇa's representatives.

Disciple: But in order for someone to surrender, doesn't he have to have faith in whoever is asking him to surrender?

Śrīla Prabhupāda: Yes, faith must be there. Therefore, in the *Bhagavad-gītā* Kṛṣṇa first of all proves that He is the Absolute Truth; then He asks you to surrender. But you need to have the intelligence to understand, "This is Kṛṣṇa"—then you surrender. In the *Bhagavad-gītā*

Kṛṣṇa does not say in the beginning, "You must surrender." First He explains everything—the body, the soul, all forms of yoga, all different kinds of knowledge. Then He gives the most confidential knowledge: "Give up everything else, and just surrender unto Me."

Everyone in this material world is imperfect. Without voluntary submission to a perfect person, everyone is imperfect. But one who has completely surrendered to Kṛṣṇa or His representative—he is perfect. But if you do not surrender to the perfect authority, then you remain an imperfect rascal. You may be Napoleon, or you may be a small ant, but we want to see whether you have surrendered to Kṛṣṇa or not. If not, then you're a rascal, that's all.

Scientific Progress: Bombastic Words

This exchange between Śrīla Prabhupāda and his disciple Bhaktisvarūpa Dāmodara Swami, Ph.D., took place in Atlanta in March of 1975.

Bhaktisvarūpa Dāmodara Swami: Modern scientists are working very hard to create life in the laboratory.
Śrīla Prabhupāda: Try to understand this: Just as God is already existing, so the living entities, being part and parcel of God, are also already existing—eternally. So you haven't got to "create." That is foolishness, because the living entities are eternal—they are never created. They simply become manifest in the material world in four different ways. Some of them are manifested through seeds, some of them through fermentation, some through eggs, and some through embryos. But the living entities are already existing, so there is no question of creation. This is the science of the living entity.

There are already so many millions and trillions of living entities, and yet the materialistic scientists are holding big conferences on how to create something. Just see this childish proposal. They are wasting time, misleading people, and wasting everyone's hard-earned money. Therefore I say they are rascals. They are trying to "create." What will they create? Everything is already there. But they do not know this, even with all their advanced education. Therefore, the *Bhagavad-gītā* describes them as *mūḍhas,* rascals.

Now, you tell these *mūḍhas,* "My dear sir, you cannot create, nor can anything be created. Just find out where the living entities are coming from, what is their source, who is the brain behind all of nature. Find that out. That is real knowledge. If you struggle for this knowledge and try to find the original source of everything, then some day you may come to the platform of *vāsudevaḥ sarvam iti sa mahātmā su-durlabhaḥ:* you'll understand that God is the source of everything, and your knowledge will be perfect."

Look at this nice flower—do you think it has come out automatically, without the direction of any brain? This is nonsensical philosophy. These so-called scientists use so many bombastic words, but how much are they actually explaining? Nobody else can understand; it is understood by them only. They put forth some complicated language in such a way that unless *they* explain it, nobody will understand. They say that everything is automatically done "by nature." That's not the fact.

Nature is an instrument, just like a wonderful computer. But still there is an operator. These rascals have no common sense. Where is the machine that is working without any operator? Is there such a machine within their experience? How can they suggest that nature is working automatically? Nature is a wonderful machine, but the operator is God, Kṛṣṇa. That is real knowledge. Just because the machine is working very wonderfully, does that mean there is no operator?

For example, the harmonium is also a machine, and if an expert musician is playing it, then it produces very melodious, pleasing sounds. "Oh, how nice." But will the harmonium play automatically and give out melodious sounds? So they don't even have any common sense, and still they are calling themselves scientists.

That is our regret: that these people don't even have any common sense, and still they are passing as scientists.

Bhaktisvarūpa Dāmodara Swami: They are thinking that because through chemistry they are able to synthesise some primitive amino adds . . .

Śrīla Prabhupāda: That is craftsmanship; that is not knowledge. For instance, let us say that you paint a picture of a rose. You are a painter, not a man of knowledge. "Man of knowledge" means someone who knows *how* things are being done. A painter simply imitates what he sees, that's all. Therefore, art and science are two different departments.

Bhaktisvarūpa Dāmodara Swami: So if they create some synthetic, that is just an art.

Śrīla Prabhupāda: Yes. For example, a good cook knows how to mix the spices and condiments and make very tasty things. So you can call a chemist a good cook. Chemistry is nothing but the art of mixing different chemicals, that's all. There is oil, there is alkaline, you mix it very professionally, and soap comes out—very useful.

Bhaktisvarūpa Dāmodara Swami: But the scientists are convinced that somehow they'll be able to create life and even make a human being.

Śrīla Prabhupāda: This is not a problem, that without your creation of life the world will go to hell. Life is already there. For instance, there are so many motorcars. If I manufacture another motorcar, is there any great credit for me? So many motorcars are already there! When there were no motorcars, the first man who manufactured one had some credit: "Yes, you have done something nice—a horseless carriage. People will benefit from it—a convenience—that's all right." But when there are millions and millions of motorcars simply creating accidents, and I manufacture another motorcar, what is my credit? What is my credit?

Bhaktisvarūpa Dāmodara Swami: Zero.

Śrīla Prabhupāda: Zero. And to achieve this zero, they are going to hold some big conference, and so many people will come and spend money.

Bhaktisvarūpa Dāmodara Swami: They want to make a better human being. They want to make life better.

Śrīla Prabhupāda: Yes, that is our proposal. We say to the scientists, "Don't waste time trying to make life. Try to make your life *better.* Try to understand what your actual spiritual identity is, so that you may become happy in this lifetime. This research should be done."

The first thing they have to learn is that there is a driver, or soul, within the "motorcar" of the body. This is the first point of knowledge. Unless one understands this simple thing, he's an ass. The driver—the soul—is moving the motorcar of this body. And if the driver is educated, then he can move his body for self-realisation, so that he can go home, back to Godhead. Then he becomes perfect. So we are educating the driver—we are not trying to manufacture another tin car. This is Kṛṣṇa consciousness.

Seeing Technology in a Spiritual Light

This exchange between Śrīla Prabhupāda and some of his disciples took place on an early-morning walk in Chicago in July of 1975.

Disciple: Earlier you were saying that the Western world is spiritually blind and that India is technologically lame, but that if they combine their resources, then both India and the West will benefit.

Śrīla Prabhupāda: Yes. If the Western world, the blind man, takes India, the lame man, on its shoulders, then the lame man can point the way spiritually and the blind man can sustain them materially, technologically. If America and India pool their technological and spiritual resources, this combination will bring about perfect peace and prosperity all over the world.

How blind these Americans are! They have attained the human form of life—such an intelligent form of life—and yet they are utilising it for riding motorboats in the lake. You see? A human being should use every moment for regaining his God consciousness. Not a single moment should be wasted—and these people are simply finding new ways to waste time.

Of course, the Americans are doing things in a very nice way, with great technological advancement, but what they are doing is *blind*. You may be a very good driver, but if you are blind, then how well will you drive? You'll create disaster. So the American people must open their eyes spiritually, so that their good driving capacity will be properly utilised. Now they're trying to see through microscopes. But as long as they remain blind to their own spiritual identity, what will they see? They may have microscopes or this machine or that machine—but *they* are blind. That they do not know.

Disciple: I think most Americans are more interested in raising a family than in self-realisation.

Śrīla Prabhupāda: Kṛṣṇa consciousness is not hindered by family life, one way or the other. *Ahaituky apratihatā.* God consciousness cannot be checked by *anything*—if you are sincere. In any circumstances you can be engaged. You can execute Kṛṣṇa consciousness in four ways: *prāṇair arthair dhiyā vācā*—by your life, by your money, by your intelligence, and by your words. So if you want to be a family man—if you cannot dedicate twenty-four hours daily—then earn money and use it to spread Kṛṣṇa consciousness. And if you cannot earn money, then use your intelligence. There is so much intellectual work to do—publication, research, and so on. If you cannot do that, then utilise your words to tell people about Kṛṣṇa. Wherever you may be, simply explain to someone, "Kṛṣṇa is the Supreme Personality of Godhead. Just offer your obeisances to Kṛṣṇa." Finished.

So where is the scarcity of opportunities? You can serve Kṛṣṇa in any capacity, provided you *want* to serve. But if you want to engage Kṛṣṇa in your service, that is a blunder. People are going to church—"God, serve us; give us our daily bread."

People manufacture their own problems. Actually, there are no problems. *Īśāvāsyam idaṁ sarvam:* God has arranged everything. He has made everything perfect and complete. You see so many fruits for the birds—so sumptuously supplied. *Pūrṇam idam:* Kṛṣṇa has already supplied everything in sufficient quantity. But these rascals are blind—they do not see this. They are trying to adjust. Why do they need to make an adjustment? Everything is already sufficient. It is just that people are misusing things. But otherwise, they already have sufficient land, sufficient intelligence—everything is sufficient.

In Africa and Australia they have so much land, but instead of relying on nature's bounty of crops, they are raising cattle to kill them. This is their intelligence. People are growing coffee and tea and tobacco, even though they know these things hurt their health. In some parts of the world people are dying for want of grain, and yet in other parts of the world people are growing tobacco, which will only bring disease and death. This is their intelligence.

The problem is that these rascals do not know that life is meant for understanding God. Ask anyone; nobody knows. They are such fools. Don't you see how much care they are taking for dogs? They're blind: they do not know whether they'll be God conscious or dog conscious. The dog runs on four legs, but people think they have become advanced because they can run by car—on four wheels. They think they have become civilised, but their business is running, that's all.

Disciple: And the purpose for the running is the same—eating, sleeping, mating, and defending.

Śrīla Prabhupāda: Yes. If the purpose is the same as a dog's, then what is the use of running by car? Of course, you can use the car for reaching people with the message of Kṛṣṇa consciousness. You can use everything for Kṛṣṇa. That is what we teach. If there is a nice car, why should I condemn it? Utilise it for Kṛṣṇa; then it is all right. We don't say, "Give it up." No. When you have produced something by your God-given intelligence, it is all right—if you use it for God. But when you use it for other purposes than Kṛṣṇa, then it is nonsense.

Take this car—so nicely decorated. If I say "It is all nonsense," is that very intelligent? No. The purpose for which you have created this car—that is nonsense. So we simply want people to change their consciousness. We don't condemn the things they have produced.

For instance, with a knife you can cut vegetables and fruit, but if you use it for cutting your throat, that is bad. So now people are using the knife of technology for cutting their own throats, for forgetting all about self-realisation, Kṛṣṇa consciousness. This is bad.

Nṛ-deham ādyaṁ su-labhaṁ su-durlabhaṁ plavaṁ su-kalpam: our human body is just like a good boat—with our human intelligence we can cross the ocean of nescience, the ocean of repeated birth and death in this material world. And *guru-karṇadhāram/ mayānukūlena nabhasvateritaṁ pumān bhavābdhiṁ na taret sa ātma-hā:* we have a favourable wind—Kṛṣṇa's instructions in the Vedic literatures—plus we have a good captain, the bona fide spiritual master, who can guide us and enlighten us. With all these facilities, if we cannot cross the ocean of nescience, then we are cutting our throats. The boat is here, the captain is here, the favourable wind is here, but we are not utilising them. That means we are killing ourselves.

The "Secular State"

This conversation between Śrīla Prabhupāda and India's ambassador to Sweden took place in Stockholm in September of 1973.

Śrīla Prabhupāda: In America and India and so many other countries all over the world, they have a "secular state." The government leaders say they don't want to favour any particular religion, but actually they are favouring irreligion.

Ambassador: Well, we have a problem. We have a multireligious society, so we people in government have to be careful. We can't take too strong a position on religion.

Śrīla Prabhupāda: No, no. The government *must* take a strong position. Of course, the government should be neutral to all forms of bona fide religion. But it also has a duty to see that the people are genuinely religious. Not that in the name of a "secular state" the government should let the people go to hell.

Ambassador: Well, that's true.

Śrīla Prabhupāda: Yes, if you are a Muslim, then it is the duty of the government to see that you are really acting as a Muslim. If you are a Hindu, it is the government's duty to see that you are acting as a Hindu. If you are Christian, it is the government's duty to see that you are acting as a Christian. The government cannot give up religion. *Dharmeṇa hīnāḥ paśubhiḥ samānāḥ:* if people become irreligious, then they are simply animals. So it is the government's duty to see that the citizens are not becoming animals. The people may profess different forms of religion. That doesn't matter. But they must be religious. "Secular state" doesn't mean that the government should be callous—"Let the people become cats and dogs, without religion." If the government doesn't care, then it isn't a good government.

Ambassador: I think there's a lot in what you say. But, you know, politics is the art of the possible.

Śrīla Prabhupāda: No. Politics means seeing that the people become advanced, that the citizens become spiritually advanced. Not that they become degraded.

Ambassador: Yes, I agree. But I think the primary duty of the government is to provide the conditions in which gifted people, spiritual leaders like you, can function. If the government does any more than that, it might even corrupt the various religious groups. I think government should be like an umpire in a game—provide the conditions for free speech.

Śrīla Prabhupāda: No. Government must do more than that. For instance, you have a commerce department—the government sees that the trade and industrial enterprises are doing nicely, working properly. The government issues licenses. They have supervisors and inspectors. Or, for instance, you have an education department—trained inspectors who see that the students are being properly educated. Similarly, the government should have expert men who can check to see that the Hindus are really acting like Hindus, the Muslims are acting like Muslims, and the Christians are acting like Christians. The government should not be callous about religion. They may be neutral. "Whatever religion you profess, we have nothing to do with that." But it is the government's duty to see that you are doing nicely—that you are not bluffing.

Ambassador: Surely . . . as far as moral conduct is concerned. But more than that, how is it possible, you know?

Śrīla Prabhupāda: The thing is, unless you are actually following religious principles, you cannot possibly have good moral conduct.

yasyāsti bhaktir bhagavaty akiñcanā
sarvair guṇais tatra samāsate surāḥ
harāv abhaktasya kuto mahad-guṇā
manorathenāsati dhāvato bahiḥ

"One who has unflinching devotion to God consistently manifests all godly qualities. But one who has no such devotion must always be concocting schemes for exploiting the Lord's material, external energy—and so he can have no good moral qualities whatsoever." [*Śrīmad-Bhāgavatam* 5.18.12]

As long as you have faith in God, devotion to God, everything is all right. After all, God is one. God is neither Hindu nor Christian nor Muslim. God is one. And that is why the Vedic literatures tell us,

sa vai puṁsāṁ paro dharmo yato bhaktir adhokṣaje
ahaituky apratihatā yayātmā suprasīdati

"The supreme duty for all humanity is to achieve loving devotional service to the Supreme Lord. Only such devotional service—unmotivated and uninterrupted—can completely satisfy the self." [*Bhāg.* 1.2.6] So one must be religious. Without being religious, no one can be satisfied. Why is there so much confusion and dissatisfaction all over the world? Because people have become irreligious.

Ambassador: In Moscow, so many people are hostile to religion, completely against it.

Śrīla Prabhupāda: Why do you say Moscow? *Everywhere.* At least in Moscow they are honest. They honestly say, "We don't believe in God."
Ambassador: That's true. That's true.
Śrīla Prabhupāda: But in other places they say, "I am Hindu," "I am Muslim," "I am Christian," "I believe in God." And still they don't know *anything* about religion. *They don't follow God's laws.*
Ambassador: I'm afraid most of us are like that. That's true.
Śrīla Prabhupāda: *[Laughs]* I should say that in Moscow at least they are gentlemen. They cannot understand religion, so they say, "We don't believe." But these other rascals say, "Yes, we're religious. In God we trust." And yet they are committing the most irreligious acts. Many times I have asked Christians, "Your Bible says, 'Thou shalt not kill.' Why are you killing?" They cannot give any satisfactory answer. It is clearly said, "Thou shalt not kill"—and they are maintaining slaughterhouses. What is this?

We Cannot Remain in Tiger Consciousness

This exchange between Śrīla Prabhupāda and some guests took place in December of 1968 at the Los Angeles Hare Kṛṣṇa centre.

Guest: If man didn't eat animals, they'd probably just die of starvation or something.

Śrīla Prabhupāda: Why are you so anxious about the animals' dying of starvation? You take care of yourself. Don't be altruistic—"Oh, they will starve. Let me eat them." What is this altruism? Kṛṣṇa is supplying food. If an animal dies of starvation, it is Kṛṣṇa's responsibility. Nobody dies of starvation. That is a false theory. Have you seen any animal dying of starvation? There is no question of starvation in the kingdom of God. We are manufacturing these theories for our own sense satisfaction. There are millions of elephants in the African jungle and Indian jungle. They require one hundred pounds at a time to eat. Who is supplying food? So there is no question of starvation in the kingdom of God. Starvation is for the so-called civilised man.

Guest: If man wasn't meant to eat meat, why in nature do the other animals kill meat?

Śrīla Prabhupāda: Are you "another animal"?

Guest: Well, we're all animals.

Śrīla Prabhupāda: You count yourself among the animals? You classify yourself with the animals?

Guest: Well, we're all animals . . .

Śrīla Prabhupāda: No, not all. You may be, but we are not. Do you like to be classified with the animals?

Guest: I don't feel that I am better than the animals. I have respect for all God's creatures.

Śrīla Prabhupāda: You have respect for all, and you kill animals?

Guest: Well, why is it—if man is not meant to eat meat—that in nature the animals eat each other?

Śrīla Prabhupāda: When animals eat meat, they are following nature's law. When you eat meat, you are breaking nature's law.

Guest: What?

Śrīla Prabhupāda: For instance, a tiger will never come to claim the grain—"Oh, you've got so much grain—give me some." No. Even if there are hundreds of bags of grain, he doesn't care. But he'll pounce upon an animal. That is his natural instinct. But why do you take grain, fruit, milk, meat, and whatever you get? What is this? You are neither animal nor human being. You are misusing your humanity! You should think, "What is eatable for *me*?" A tiger may eat meat—he is a tiger. But I am not a tiger; I am a human being. If I've got enough grain, fruit, vegetables, and other things God has given; why should I go to kill a poor animal? This is humanity.

You are animal plus human. If you forget your humanity, then you are an animal. *[A brief silence]* So we are not simply animals. We are animal plus human. If we increase our quality of humanity, then our life is perfect. But if we remain in animality, then our life is imperfect. So we have to increase our human consciousness—that is Kṛṣṇa consciousness. If you can live very peacefully, very nicely, in good health by eating so many varieties of vegetarian foods given by Kṛṣṇa, why should you kill an animal?

Besides that, scientifically, your teeth are meant for

eating vegetables. The tiger has teeth for eating meat. Nature has made it like that. He has to kill another animal; therefore he has nails, he has teeth, he has strength. But you have no such strength. You cannot kill a cow like that—pouncing like a tiger. You have to make a slaughterhouse and sit down at your home. If somebody else slaughters the cow, you can eat very nicely. What is this? Do like the tiger! Pounce upon a cow and eat! You cannot do that.

Guest: So you don't believe in nature's law. I believe nature's law applies equally to everybody.

Śrīla Prabhupāda: The tiger is made by nature's law in that way, so therefore he can do that. You cannot do it—your nature is different. You have discrimination, you have conscience, you are claiming to be a civilised human being—so you should utilise all this. That is Kṛṣṇa consciousness, perfect consciousness. Human life is meant for raising oneself to the perfection of consciousness, and that is Kṛṣṇa consciousness. We cannot remain in tiger consciousness. That is not humanity.

Another guest: Have we fallen from higher to lower, or have we come up from plants and animals?

Śrīla Prabhupāda: Yes, naturally you have fallen from higher to lower—from the spiritual world to this material world, and then down to the lower species. Then you make progress, and you again come to this human form. If you utilise your higher consciousness, then you go still higher: you go to God. But if you don't use your higher consciousness, you again go down.

So don't be misguided. Take to God consciousness, Kṛṣṇa consciousness, and that will be proper use of this human form of life. Otherwise, if we indulge in meat-eating like a tiger, we may get the body of a tiger in our next life, but what is the use? Suppose I become a very strong tiger in my next life. Is that a very good promotion? Do you know the life of a tiger? They cannot even eat daily. They pounce upon one animal and keep it secretly, and for a month they eat the decomposed flesh—because they don't always get the chance to kill an animal. God will not give that chance. It is natural: in the jungle, wherever there is a tiger the other animals flee. Self-defence. So on rare occasions, when the tiger is too hungry, then God gives him a chance to pounce upon another animal. A tiger cannot get so many palatable dishes daily. It is in the human form of life that we have all these facilities. But if we misuse them, then . . . go to the tiger's life. Be very strong, with full pouncing capacity.

The God-Blind Scientists

The following conversation between Śrīla Prabhupāda and some of his disciples took place in December of 1973 during an early-morning walk at Venice Beach, in Los Angeles.

Disciple: The scientists say their power of reason tells them there's no God. They say if you believe in God it's strictly a matter of faith.
Śrīla Prabhupāda: It is not a matter of faith—it is fact.
Disciple: When scientists say "fact," they mean something they can perceive through their senses.
Śrīla Prabhupāda: Yes, and in Kṛṣṇa consciousness we can perceive God through our senses. The more we engage our senses in devotional service—service to God—the more we are able to perceive Him. *Hṛṣīkeṇa hṛṣīkeśa-sevanaṁ bhaktir ucyate:* "When one engages his senses in service to the Supreme, that relationship is called *bhakti* [devotion]." For example, we use our legs to walk to the temple, and our tongue to glorify God and eat *prasādam* ["the Lord's mercy," vegetarian food offered to Kṛṣṇa].
Disciple: But the scientists say these are acts of faith. They say that when we offer food to God, it's only our faith that makes us think God accepts it. They say *they* can't see Him eating.
Śrīla Prabhupāda: *They* cannot see, but *I* can see. I am not a fool like them. They are spiritually blind—suffering from cataracts, ignorance. If they come to me, I shall operate, and then they'll see God also.
Disciple: Well, the scientists want to see God now.

Śrīla Prabhupāda: But Kṛṣṇa will not reveal Himself to them now, because they're rascals—big animals. *Śva-viḍ-varāhoṣṭra-kharaiḥ saṁstutaḥ puruṣaḥ paśuḥ:* "Anyone who's not a devotee of God is just a big animal—a big camel or a big dog or a big swine—and the people who praise him are the same."

Disciple: They say we're just dreamers—that we make up fantasies about God and the spiritual world.

Śrīla Prabhupāda: Why do they say "fantasies"? They have no brain to understand—so they say "fantasies."

Disciple: Well, their standard of objectivity is what they can perceive through their senses.

Śrīla Prabhupāda: Yes, they can perceive God through their senses. When they perceive sand through their senses, who do they think made the sand? *They* didn't. When they perceive the ocean through their senses, who do they think made that? Why are they such fools that they don't understand this?

Disciple: They say that if God made these things, they'd be able to see Him, just as they can see the ocean.

Śrīla Prabhupāda: And I say to them, "Yes, you can see God—but first you have to have the eyes. You are blind; you have cataracts. Come to me and I will operate. Then you'll see God." This is why the Vedic scriptures say, *tad vijñānārthaṁ sa gurum evābhigacchet:* "To see God, you must approach a bona fide spiritual master." Otherwise, how can they see God with their blind eyes?

Disciple: But the scientists don't have any faith in the kind of seeing you're talking about. The only kind of seeing they put any faith in is what they can gather through their eyes and their microscopes and telescopes.

Śrīla Prabhupāda: Why? If you look up in the sky now, you will think it is vacant. But it is not vacant—your eyes are deficient. There are innumerable planets and stars in the sky, but you cannot see them—you are blind to them. So just because you cannot see the stars and planets, does this mean they do not exist?

Disciple: The scientists admit they're ignorant about some things. But still they won't accept your explanation of things they can't see with their own eyes.

Śrīla Prabhupāda: Why not?

Disciple: Because they think that what you tell them may be wrong.

Śrīla Prabhupāda: That is their misfortune. Our gross senses cannot approach God. To know Him we have to hear from an authority—that is the process for gaining higher knowledge.

Disciple: But that step requires faith. Faith in the guru.

Śrīla Prabhupāda: Not faith—common sense! If you want to learn medicine, you have to go to an expert physician. You cannot learn it by yourself.

Disciple: Śrīla Prabhupāda, from all you've said, it's obvious we can support our ideas as well as the atheistic scientists can support theirs. But they're in control of society. They're dominant.

Śrīla Prabhupāda: Dominant? [*Laughs*] One kick from Māyā [Kṛṣṇa's material energy] and all their "dominance" is finished in one second. They are controlled by Māyā, but they are thinking that they are free. This is foolishness.

Disciple: They don't want to come to their senses.

Śrīla Prabhupāda: Therefore they are rascals. A rascal is someone who will insist he's right even after you have proved he's wrong. He will never take a good lesson. And why do they remain rascals? *Na māṁ duṣkṛtino mūḍhāḥ prapadyante narādhamāḥ:* because they are *duṣkṛtina*—very, very sinful. Don't you see how they are making a world of slaughterhouses and brothels, how they are ruining everyone's life by promoting sensual enjoyment? These are all sinful activities. And because the scientists are so sinful, they will have to suffer in the darkest regions of hell. In their next life they'll become worms in stool. Yet out of ignorance they are thinking they are safe.

Give God the Nobel Prize

The following conversation between Śrīla Prabhupāda and some of his disciples took place on an early-morning walk in Geneva in June of 1974.

Śrīla Prabhupāda: Just look at this fig. In this one fig you find thousands of seeds—and each tiny seed is a whole new fig tree.

Now, where is that chemist who can do such a thing: First make a tree, and then make the tree bear fruit, and next make the fruit produce seeds, and finally make the seeds produce still more trees? Just tell me. Where is that chemist?

Disciple: They talk very proudly, Śrīla Prabhupāda, but none of these chemists and such can do any of these things.

Śrīla Prabhupāda: Once a big chemist came to me and admitted, "Our chemical advancement, our scientific advancement, is like a man who has learned to bark. So many natural dogs are already barking, but no one pays any attention. But if a man artificially learns the art of barking, oh, so many people will go to see—and even purchase tickets for ten dollars, twenty dollars. Just to see an artificial dog. Our scientific advancement is like this."

If a man makes an artificial imitation of nature, say by barking, people go to see and even pay money. When it comes to the natural barking, no one cares. And when these big so-called scientific rascals claim they can manufacture life, people give all sorts of praise and awards. As for God's perfect, natural process—millions and millions of beings born at each moment—no one cares. People don't give God's process very much credit.

The fool who concocts some utopian scheme for creating living beings from dead material chemicals—he is given all credit, you see: the Nobel Prize. "Oh, here is a creative genius." And nature is injecting millions and millions of souls into material bodies at every moment—the arrangement of God—and no one cares. This is rascaldom.

Even if we suppose you *could* manufacture a man or animal in your laboratory, what would be your credit? After all, a single man or animal created by you, and millions and millions created by the Lord. So we want to give credit to Kṛṣṇa, who is really creating all these living beings we see every day.

Disciple: Śrīla Prabhupāda, you remember Aldous Huxley, who predicted in *Brave New World* a process of genetically screening babies, of breeding men for certain traits. The idea would be to take one strain of traits and breed a class of workingmen, take another strain of traits and breed a class of administrators, and take still another strain of traits and breed a class of cultured advisers and scholars.

Śrīla Prabhupāda: Once again, that is already present in God's natural arrangement. *Guṇa-karma-vibhāgaśaḥ:* according to one's qualities and activities in his past life, in this present life he gets a fitting body. If one has cultivated the qualities and activities of ignorance, he gets an ignorant body and must live by manual labour. If one has cultivated the qualities and activities of striving passion, he gets a passionate body and must live by taking charge of others—administration. If one has cultivated the qualities and activities of enlightenment, he gets an enlightened body and must live by enlightening and advising others.

So you see, God has already made such a perfect arrangement. Every soul receives the body he desires and deserves, and the social order receives citizens with required traits. Not that you have to breed these traits. By His natural arrangement, the Lord equips a particular soul with particular kinds of bodies. Why even try imitating what God and nature already do perfectly?

I told that scientist who visited me, "You scientists—you are simply wasting time." Childish. They are just imitating the dog's barking. The scientist pays no attention, gives no credit to the real dog doing the real barking. Actually, that is today's situation. When the natural dog barks, that is not science. When the artificial, imitation dog barks, that is science. Isn't it so? To whatever degree the scientist succeeds in artificially imitating what the Lord's natural arrangement is already doing—that is science.

Disciple: Śrīla Prabhupāda, when you heard about the scientists' claiming they can now produce babies in a test tube, you said, "But that is already being done in the mother's womb. The womb is the perfect test tube."

Śrīla Prabhupāda: Yes. Nature is already doing everything with utter perfection. But some puffed-up scientist will make a shabby imitation—using the ingredients nature supplies—and get the Nobel Prize. And what to speak of actually creating a baby—let us see the scientists produce even one blade of grass in their proud laboratories.

Disciple: They should give the Lord and Mother Nature the Nobel Prize.

Śrīla Prabhupāda: Yes, yes.

Disciple: Really, I think they should give you the Nobel

Prize. You've taken so many foolish atheists and created devotees of God.

Śrīla Prabhupāda: Oh, I—I am a "natural dog," so they'll not give me any prize. *[Laughs]* They will award the prize to the artificial dogs.

On Social Revolution

The following conversation between Śrīla Prabhupāda and members of the United Nations World Health Organization took place in Geneva in June of 1974.

Śrīla Prabhupāda: All over the world, or anywhere in the world, you can make this experiment, just as we are doing. Live very simply, be self-sufficient; get your necessities not from factories but from the farmland. And glorify God's holy names.

In this industrial setup, capitalist or communist, only a few big men can be happy—so-called happy—at the expense of the other people. And because the others are being exploited or simply left unemployed by this corrupt few, the others also become corrupt. They try to avoid all work and sit idly. Or else they do not work honestly. And so many other things.

So the only remedy is that everyone should live naturally and chant God's holy names. Become God conscious. This remedy is simple, and here you can see some of the results. My young European and American students, they had been addicted to drugs and drinking and smoking and so many other modern bad habits. But now, just see how sober they are and how they are glorifying the Lord's holy names.

You can change the world and make everything all right, provided you take this instruction. There is no other remedy. If you choose not to listen, what can be done? The remedy—the right medicine—is there. But if you don't take the medicine, how will the disease be cured?

W.H.O. member: You referred earlier to the unfortunate departure of villagers to the city. You pointed out that in city life the villagers become factory workers, and then so many evils follow. And you suggested as a solution that if we live in the village and work the land for a mere three months, we'll have food to eat for the whole year.

But I'd like to point out that there is such a vast amount of unemployment in our towns and villages. Many people there are feeling doomed. They cannot produce enough food for themselves, because they do not have access to the land. The mercantile people use it for their own purposes. And this is why so many of the ordinary people are unemployed. This is why they go into the cities. It is not necessarily that "the good life" in the city attracts them, but that they don't have access to the land. The land is not used by the mercantile group, and the ordinary people are not able to live in the villages as free men and grow enough food for themselves.

Now, the mercantile group are exploiting. They are exploiting. So unless there is some kind of revolution by which you can curb the power of this mercantile group, how can you hope that someday people will be able to live in their villages and grow their own food on the land?

Śrīla Prabhupāda: The thing is, the government has the duty to see that nobody is unemployed. That is good government. In the Vedic system, society has four natural groupings. The *brāhmaṇas,* or thoughtful group, instruct and advise. The *kṣatriyas,* or dynamic group, protect and organise. Then the *vaiśyas,* or mercantile group, look after the land and cows and see to food production. And the *śūdras,* or labouring group, assist the other groups.

Now, this means that the government should be composed of dynamic *kṣatriyas* who will protect everyone else and make sure the various groupings are doing their duties. The government has to see that everyone is properly employed. Then the whole problem of unemployment will be solved.

W.H.O. member: But at present the mercantile group are also in the government. In fact, they are entrenched. They have a very strong voice in the government, and in many instances they are outright officials in the government.

Śrīla Prabhupāda: No—that means bad government.

W.H.O. member: Yes, that is . . . that is true.

Śrīla Prabhupāda: That is bad government. The mercantile group should have nothing to do with the government. Otherwise, how can the government see—with no ulterior motives—about everyone's employment?

The government should encourage the mercantile group to use their ingenuity freely, but not to devise unnatural industries that come and go and leave people unemployed. The government has to see that everyone is properly employed.

W.H.O. member: That's what I am looking forward to—the day when the Kṛṣṇa consciousness movement can become a real revolutionary movement that will change the face of society.

Śrīla Prabhupāda: Yes. I think it will bring revolution, because the American and European people are taking it to heart. I have introduced it to them, and they're very intelligent—they take everything very seriously.

We have been working only a few years, and yet we have spread this movement all over the world. If people take it seriously, it will go on, and there will be revolution. Because we are not working whimsically, capriciously. We are taking authoritative direction from the *śāstra,* the scripture. There is so much information here. People can read all these books and get information. If they take it seriously, it will bring revolution.

W.H.O. member: There is one thing that I cannot reconcile. As an Indian, the question bothers me very, very often. I believe in a great many things that you said about returning to a simpler, more natural way of life, and about finding satisfaction in our spiritual dimension. There's no question about that. I'm not what you would call a "Westernized Indian." But what I cannot reconcile is the fact that we who had this spiritual knowledge and all our cultural guidelines, which you have just now said are the solutions to all our problems—with all these guidelines we have not been able to keep our society free from so many evils that have come about. I'm referring not only to the poverty but also to the unemployment and to the hunger and to many other things.

Śrīla Prabhupāda: No. It is not because of our cultural guidelines, but because of bad leaders who do not follow them. It is due to these bad leaders.

W.H.O. member: They are our own people. They . . .

Śrīla Prabhupāda: They may be our own people. They may be our own *father.* Prahlāda Mahārāja was a devotee of the Lord, and yet his father was Hiraṇyakaśipu, an utter demon. So what can be done? Most people are good, and yet so often we see that their leader is a godless demon.

W.H.O. member: Yes. Hiraṇyakaśipu had to be destroyed.

Śrīla Prabhupāda: So he was destroyed. By God's grace he was destroyed. And every one of these modern demonic leaders—they will be destroyed. They'll be destroyed. But everything takes time.

At the present moment, our leaders are not very

good. Blind. They have no knowledge, and yet they are leading. *Andhā yathāndhair upanīyamānās:* the blind leading the blind—into the ditch. These leaders have killed the world's original, spiritual culture, and they cannot give anything in its place.

W.H.O. member: So has your movement involved itself in social philosophy, then?

Śrīla Prabhupāda: Yes. This movement is most practical. For instance, we are recommending no meat-eating. And the leaders do not like it. We are not very favourable to their propaganda. So the leaders don't like us. After all, they have allowed slaughterhouses and beef shops anywhere and everywhere, and we are saying, "No meat-eating." So how will they like us? That is the difficulty. "It is folly to be wise where ignorance is bliss." But still we are struggling.

And the alternative we are recommending is also practical. These God conscious farming villages have proved successful. The inhabitants are finding their lives happy and abundant. Nature's bounty supplies fruit and vegetables and grain. And the cows supply milk, from which you can get yogurt, cheese, butter, and cream. So with all these ingredients, you can make hundreds and thousands of delicious preparations. And you feel fully satisfied. That is the basic principle.

W.H.O. member: That is an example of a successful enterprise, but would you speak about something now that has not been tried before?

Śrīla Prabhupāda: The "new thing" is that these people living in God conscious farming villages do not have to travel away for their daily bread. That is the new thing for modern society.

At present, most people have to travel some distance to the factory or office. I happened to be in Bombay when there was a railway strike—oh, people were suffering so much. You see? From five o'clock in the morning they were standing in a queue for catching a train. Of course, during the strike hardly any trains were running. So people were in so much difficulty. And if one or two trains were running, so many people were trying to squeeze themselves into the cars. Smashing themselves in. They were even on top of the train.

Of course, in the more industrially advanced countries, the people go to the factory or office in cars—and risk being killed in highway crashes. So the question is, Why should one be induced to go so many miles away from his home simply for earning his livelihood? This is a very bad civilisation. One must obtain food locally. That is a good civilisation.

W.H.O. member: I understand that your goal is to have everybody become self-sufficient in regard to food. But if all the people are engaged in the production of food, then who will be providing other things?

Śrīla Prabhupāda: We don't say everyone should be engaged in food production. According to the *Bhagavad-gītā,* naturally you will have a section of men who will produce food, a section of men who will give spiritual direction, and a section of men who will manage as the government or king. And the rest of the people are labourers who help all the other sections.

It is not that everyone will be a cultivator. No. There must also be a brain department, a management department, and a worker department. These groupings are natural within any society. And all of them should work together for spiritual cultivation.

Colleges for Curing the Social Body

This conversation between Śrīla Prabhupāda and some of his disciples took place in Vṛndāvana, India, in March of 1974.

Śrīla Prabhupāda: In this age the politicians' business will be to exploit the poor citizens, and the citizens will be embarrassed and harassed so much. On one side there will be insufficient rain and therefore scarcity of food, and on the other side there will be excessive taxation by the government. In this way the people will be so much harassed that they will give up their homes and go to the forest.

Ātreya Ṛṣi Dāsa: Nowadays the government simply collects money and does nothing.

Śrīla Prabhupāda: The government's duty is to see that every person is employed according to his capacity. There should be no unemployment—that is a very dangerous situation in society. But the government has drawn people off the land and into the cities. The philosophy of the government officials seems to be, "What is the use of so many people working on the land? Instead we can kill animals and eat them." It's all very easy, because today people don't care about the law of *karma*, the inevitable results of sinful activities. "If we can eat the cows, why should we take so much trouble to till the land?" This is going on all over the world.

Ātreya Ṛṣi Dāsa: Yes, the farmers' sons are giving up farming and going to the city.

Śrīla Prabhupāda: You know this nonsense of "topless, bottomless"? The leaders want that. They want the hotels to pick up college girls and let them be enjoyed by the guests. All over the world the whole population is becoming polluted. So how can people expect good government? Some of the people will take charge of the government, but they are polluted.

So wherever we have a Hare Kṛṣṇa centre we should immediately establish a college for training people—first, according to their natural talents [intellectual, administrative, productive, and labouring]. And everyone will be elevated to spiritual awareness by performing the spiritual activities we prescribe—chanting the Hare Kṛṣṇa mantra, hearing the science of self-realisation from the *Bhagavad-gītā,* and doing everything as an offering to Kṛṣṇa. Everyone's life will become devotional service to the supreme Lord.

At the same time, for the management of practical affairs we have to organise and train the different social divisions, because there are different kinds of brains. Those who have very intellectual brains should become *brāhmaṇas:* priests, teachers, advisers. Those who are fit for management and protection of others should become *kṣatriyas:* administrators and military men. Those who are fit for producing food and taking care of the cows should become *vaiśyas,* mercantile men. And those who can assist the others and take up trades and crafts should become *śūdras,* workingmen.

In the social body, just as in your own body, there must be divisions of work. If everyone wants to be the brain [the intellectuals] or the arms [the administrators], then who is going to act as the belly [the farmers] or the legs [the manual workers]? Every kind of occupation is needed. The brain is needed, the arms are needed, the belly is needed, the legs are needed. So you will have to organise the social body. You have to help people understand the Supreme Lord's natural social divisions: some people will work as the brain, others as the arms, others as the belly, and still others as the legs. The main aim is to keep the social body perfectly fit.

You must make sure that everyone can engage in the kind of occupation he is suited for. That is important. The thing is, every kind of work can be devotional service to the Lord—the main point is to see that people are engaged in that spirit in their natural work. For instance, when you are walking, your brain is working—"Go this way; go that way; a car is coming"—and your brain says to your legs, "Come to this side." Now, the work of the brain and the work of the legs are different, but the central point is one—to get you safely across the street. Similarly, the central point of the social body should be one—everyone should help in serving Kṛṣṇa.

Satsvarūpa Dāsa Gosvāmī: Will this kind of college be for the general public?

Śrīla Prabhupāda: Yes, for anyone. For instance, an engineering college is open for everyone; the only requirement is that people must be ready to take up the training. This is our most important program now, because people all over the world have been misguided by these so-called leaders. Children can attend a Kṛṣṇa-conscious primary school, and then, when they are grown up, they can attend a Kṛṣṇa-conscious college for further development in their occupational work and their devotional life.

Ātreya Ṛṣi Dāsa: Will we teach business also?

Śrīla Prabhupāda: Not this modern business—no. That is rascaldom. Business means that you produce enough grain and other crops so that you can eat sumptuously and distribute to everyone—men and animals (especially the cows)—so that they will become stout and strong. That way the cows can supply milk and the human community can work hard, without suffering from disease. We are not going to open mills and factories. No.

Yaduvara Dāsa: Śrīla Prabhupāda, what class do the arts and crafts come under? In modern society artists and musicians are accepted as philosophers.

Śrīla Prabhupāda: No. An artist is a workingman. At the present moment your colleges and universities are placing too much stress on the arts and crafts. Therefore the whole population is workingmen. No real philosopher, no wisdom. That is the difficulty. Everyone is being drawn by the attraction of getting a high salary. They take a so-called technical or scientific education and end up working in a factory. Of course, they won't work in the field to produce crops. Such people are not philosophers. A philosopher is one who is searching out the Absolute Truth.

In your Western countries the rascals are writing about the philosophy of sex, which is known to the dog. This kind of philosophy can be appreciated by rascals, but we do not appreciate it. Someone who is searching after the Absolute Truth—he is a philosopher. Not this rascal Freud—elaborating on how to have sex. In the Western countries the people have all become low class, and Freud has become their philosopher. "In the jungle, the jackal becomes the king." That's all.

What is the actual knowledge in this so-called Western philosophy? The whole Western world is struggling along for industry, for making money—"Eat, drink, and be merry," wine and women. That's all. They are less than low class. This is the first time the attempt is being made to make them human beings. Don't mind that I am using very strong words—it is a fact. They are animals, two-legged animals. Rejected men. Vedic civilisation rejects them as the lowest of the low. But they can be reclaimed.

Westerners can be reclaimed, just as you Westerners—my students—have been reclaimed. Although you come from the lowest situation, by training you are becoming more than *brāhmaṇas*. There is no bar to anyone. But unfortunately, these rascals do not agree to accept this opportunity. As soon as you say "No more illicit sex, no more meat-eating," they become angry. Rascals and fools. As soon as you give them good lessons—education—they become angry. If you give a snake nice milk and banana, the result is that he will simply increase his poison.

But somehow, by Kṛṣṇa's grace, you are becoming trained. *You* become trained and revise the whole pattern of Western civilisation, especially in America. Then a new chapter will come in. This is the program. Therefore Kṛṣṇa conscious colleges are required.

His Divine Grace A. C. Bhaktivedanta Swami Prabhupāda
Founder-*Ācārya* of the International Society for Krishna Consciousness

The Author

His Divine Grace A. C. Bhaktivedanta Swami Prabhupāda appeared in this world in 1896 in Calcutta, India. He first met his spiritual master, Śrīla Bhaktisiddhānta Sarasvatī Gosvāmī, in Calcutta in 1922. Bhaktisiddhānta Sarasvatī, a prominent religious scholar and the founder of sixty-four Gauḍīya Maṭhas (Vedic institutes), liked this educated young man and convinced him to dedicate his life to teaching Vedic knowledge. Śrīla Prabhupāda became his student and, in 1933, his formally initiated disciple.

At their first meeting, in 1922, Śrīla Bhaktisiddhānta Sarasvatī requested Śrīla Prabhupāda to broadcast Vedic knowledge in English. In the years that followed, Śrīla Prabhupāda wrote a commentary on the *Bhagavad-gītā,* assisted the Gauḍīya Maṭha in its work, and, in 1944, started *Back to Godhead,* an English fortnightly magazine. Single-handedly, Śrīla Prabhupāda edited it, typed the manuscripts, checked the galley proofs, and even distributed the individual copies. The magazine is now being continued by his disciples in the West.

In 1950 Śrīla Prabhupāda retired from married life, adopting the *vānaprastha* (retired) order to devote more time to his studies and writing. He travelled to the holy city of Vṛndāvana, where he lived in humble circumstances in the historic temple of Rādhā-Dāmodara. There he engaged for several years in deep study and writing. He accepted the renounced order of life (*sannyāsa*) in 1959. At Rādhā-Dāmodara, Śrīla

Prabhupāda began work on his life's masterpiece: a multivolume commentated translation of the eighteen-thousand-verse *Śrīmad-Bhāgavatam* (*Bhāgavata Purāṇa*). He also wrote *Easy Journey to Other Planets.*

After publishing three volumes of the *Bhāgavatam,* Śrīla Prabhupāda came to the United States, in September 1965, to fulfil the mission of his spiritual master. Subsequently, His Divine Grace wrote more than fifty volumes of authoritative commentated translations and summary studies of the philosophical and religious classics of India.

When he first arrived by freighter in New York City, Śrīla Prabhupāda was practically penniless. Only after almost a year of great difficulty did he establish the International Society for Krishna Consciousness, in July of 1966. Before he passed away on November 14, 1977, he had guided the Society and seen it grow to a worldwide confederation of more than one hundred *āśramas,* schools, temples, institutes, and farm communities.

In 1972 His Divine Grace introduced the Vedic system of primary and secondary education in the West by founding the *gurukula* school in Dallas, Texas. Since then his disciples have established similar schools throughout the United States and the rest of the world.

Śrīla Prabhupāda also inspired the construction of several large international cultural centres in India. The centre at Śrīdhāma Māyāpur is the site for a planned spiritual city, an ambitious project for which construction will extend over many years to come. In Vṛndāvana are the magnificent Kṛṣṇa-Balarāma Temple and International Guesthouse, *gurukula* school, and Śrīla Prabhupāda Memorial and Museum. There is also a major cultural and educational centre in Bombay. Other centres are planned in a dozen important locations on the Indian subcontinent.

Śrīla Prabhupāda's most significant contribution, however, is his books. Highly respected by scholars for their authority, depth, and clarity, they are used as textbooks in numerous college courses. His writings have been translated into over fifty languages. The Bhaktivedanta Book Trust, established in 1972 to publish the works of His Divine Grace, has thus become the world's largest publisher of books in the field of Indian religion and philosophy.

In just twelve years, in spite of his advanced age, Śrīla Prabhupāda circled the globe fourteen times on lecture tours that took him to six continents. In spite of such a vigorous schedule, Śrīla Prabhupāda continued to write prolifically. His writings constitute a veritable library of Vedic philosophy, religion, literature, and culture.

On Transliterated Sanskrit Words

Words in italic typeface are transliterated Sanskrit terms from the original text.

In this book there are many Sanskrit terms that have no convenient English alternative. These specialized terms pose a difficulty for the reader new to Srila Prabhupada's books. The following gives an indication of how to pronounce these terms.

In Sanskrit and Bengali, the vowels are pronounced almost as in Italian. The sound of the short **a** is like the **u** in b**u**t, the long **ā** is like the **a** in f**a**r and held twice as long as the short **a**, and **e** is pronounced like the **a** in ev**a**de. The short **i** is like the **i** in **i**t; the long **ī** is like **i** in p**i**que and, like the long **ā**, held twice as long as the short **i**. The vowel **ṛ** is rolled with the tip of the tongue, like the **r** in Spanish and Italian. The **c** is pronounced like the **ch** in the word **ch**air, and the aspirated consonants (**ch**, **jh**, **dh**, etc.) are pronounced as staun**ch-h**eart, hed**ge-h**og, re**d-h**ot, etc. The compound consonant **jñ** is pronounced like the English **gy**. The **ṣ** or **ś** is pronounced like the English **sh**.

Index

God (*continued*)
living entities part of, 84
love for, 38
material world made by, 98
Māyāvādīs against, 48
Māyāvādīs not, 48
name and address of, 75
and Nobel Prize, 101, 103
offering food to, 97
orders of, 66
as operator of nature, 82
perceivable through senses, 98
perceived via Kṛṣṇa consciousness, 97
as perfect & complete, 86
seen via approaching spiritual master, 98
service to, 97
sinful cannot understand, 38
as source of everything, 82
as Supreme, 79
surrender to, 48
trust in, 75, 92
as ultimate destination, 95
unapproachable via gross senses, 99
understanding, 87, 102
why He creates world, 9
Government, 66, 76–77, 106–107, 110
bad, 107, 111
good, 78
not separate from God, 76
one-world, 54
religious duty of, 89, 90, 111
Government (*continued*)
secular, 89
single mothers supported by, 42
and *vaiśyas,* 107

Hare Kṛṣṇa
chanting of, 27–28, 60, 69, 112
movement, 118

Ignorance, 47, 55–56, 68, 109
activities in, 102
as cause of sin, 53
compared to cataracts, 97
complacency result of, 100
empiricism as, 11
"rabbit philosophy" as, 59
voidism as, 10
Intoxication, 23, 69, 75

Karma, 20, 50–51, 62, 74, 102, 111
ugra-, 25
Killing, 38
abortion as, 19, 44, 74
by Christians, 92
in slaughterhouses, 22
animals, 37, 69, 71–72
cows, 38, 54
humans, 72
necessary sometimes, 38
oneself, 88
vegetables, 71–72

Centres of the International Society for Krishna Consciousness

Founder-*Ācārya:* His Divine Grace
A. C. Bhaktivedanta Swami Prabhupāda

UNITED KINGDOM AND IRELAND

For further information on classes, programmes, festivals, residential courses and local meetings, please contact the centre nearest you.

Belfast – Sri Sri Radha-Madhava Mandir, Brooklands, 140 Upper Dunmurray Lane, Belfast, BT17 0HE / Tel: +44 (0)28 9062 0530

Birmingham – 84 Stanmore Rd, Edgbaston, Birmingham, B16 9TB / Tel: +44 (0)121 420 4999

Coventry – Kingfield Rd, Coventry (mail: 19 Gloucester St, Coventry CV1 3BZ) / Tel: +44 (0)24 7655 2822 or 5420
E-mail: haridas.kds@pamho.net

Dublin – Chaitanya Centre, 24 Thorncastle St., Dublin 2, Ireland
Tel: +353 (0)1 668 3767 / E-mail: uddhava@eircom.net

Leicester – 21 Thoresby St, North Evington, Leicester, LE5 4GU
Tel & Fax: +44 (0)116 236 7723 or 276 2587 / Mobile: +44 (0)7887 560260 / E-mail: gauranga.sundara@pamho.net

Liverpool – 114 Bold St, Liverpool, L1 4HY
Tel: +44 (0)1555 894790 / E-mail: karunabhavan@aol.com

London (central) – Sri Sri Radha-Krishna Temple, 10 Soho St, London, W1D 3DL / Tel: +44 (0)20 7437 3662, Fax: +44 (0)20 7439 1127 / E-mail: london@pamho.net / Web: www.iskcon-london.com

London (north) – Bhaktivedanta Manor, Hilfield Lane, Watford, WD25 8EZ / Tel: +44 (0)1923 857244 / Fax: +44 (0)1923 852896

London (south) – 42 Enmore Rd, South Norwood, London, SE25 5NG / Tel: +44 (0)20 8656 4296

Manchester – 20 Mayfield Rd, Whalley Range, Manchester, M16 8FT
Tel: +44 (0)161 226 4416, Tel & Fax: +44 (0)161 860 6117
E-mail: iskcon_manchester@hotmail.com

Newcastle-upon-Tyne – 304 Westgate Rd, Newcastle-upon-Tyne, NE4 6AR / Tel: +44 (0)191 272 1911 / E-mail: bhakti.rasa@pamho.net

Plymouth – 2 Windermere Crescent, Derriford, Plymouth, PL6 5HX
Tel: +44 (0)1752 776708 / E-mail: dhirasanta@aol.com

Romford – 3 Rowan Walk, Hornchurch, Romford, RM11 2JA
Tel: +44 (0)1708 454092

Scotland – Karuna Bhavan, Bankhouse Rd, Lesmahagow, Lanarkshire, ML11 0ES / Tel: +44 (0)1555 894790
Fax: +44 (0)1555 894526 / E-mail: karunabhavan@aol.com

RURAL COMMUNITIES

Upper Lough Erne (Northern Ireland) – Govindadwipa Dhama, Inisrath Island, Derrylin, Co. Fermanagh, BT92 9GN
Tel: +44 (0)28 6772 1512 / E-mail: govindadwipa@pamho.net

RESTAURANTS

Dublin – Govinda's, 4 Aungier St, Dublin 2, Ireland
Tel: +353 (0)1 475 0309 / E-mail: pragosa@connect.ie

London – Govinda's, 10 Soho St, London, W1D 3DL
Tel: +44 (0)20 7437 4928

Swansea – Govinda's, 8 Craddock St, Swansea, SA1 3EN
Tel: +44 (0)1792 468469 / E-mail: govin_das@hotmail.com

Visit us on the web:
www.iskcon.org
www.gouranga.cc

and for UK info and projects:
www.iskcon.org.uk
www.iskcon-london.com